Communication policies in **Brazil**

Communication policies in **Brazil**

A study carried out by
Nelly de Camargo and Virgilio B. Noya Pinto

The Unesco Press
Paris 1975

Published by the Unesco Press,
7 Place de Fontenoy, 75700 Paris
Printed by S.C. Maison d'Édition, Marcinelle (Belgium)

ISBN 92-3-101296-7

Preface

Communication policies are sets of principles and norms established to guide the behaviour of communication systems. They are shaped over time in the context of society's general approach to communication and to the media. Emanating from political ideologies, the social and economic conditions of the country and the values on which they are based, they strive to relate these to the real needs for and the prospective opportunities of communication.

Communication policies exist in every society, though they may sometimes be latent and disjointed, rather than clearly articulated and harmonized. They may be very general, in the nature of desirable goals and principles, or they may be more specific and practically binding. They may exist or be formulated at many levels. They may be incorporated in the constitution or legislation of a country; in over-all national policies, in the guidelines for individual administrations, in professional codes of ethics as well as in the constitutions and operational rules of particular communication institutions.

The publication of this series of studies has been undertaken as part of the programme adopted by the General Conference of Unesco at its sixteenth session, related to the analysis of communication policies as they exist at the different levels—public, institional, professional—in selected countries. The aim of the series is to present this information in a manner which can be comparable. Thus an attempt has been made to follow, as far as possible, a fairly similar structural pattern and method of approach which was agreed between the national institutions undertaking the work.

This survey of communication policies in Brazil has been carried out by Nelly de Camargo and Virgilio B. Noya Pinto, from the University of São Paulo, at the request of the Brazilian National Commission for Unesco. The opinions expressed by the authors do not necessarily reflect the views of Unesco.

Acknowledgements

This study was prepared at the request of the Brazilian National Commission for Unesco, Instituto Brasileiro de Educação, Ciência e Cultura, (IBECC).

The authors are indebted to the many government officials, managers and staff members of mass media enterprises, jurists and eminent personalities in the fields of communication and politics who gave so generously of their time and views. The opinions expressed in the study are, however, the authors' own.

Special reference should be made to Flávic Q. de Moraes Jr, Professor of Ethics of Journalism, Jan Koudela, Professor of Cinema Legislation, and two former students, Mario de Conceição Lemes da Silva and Maria J. Bressan, who collected data. The University of São Paulo acted as the Brazilian sponsoring institution for the project.

Nelly de Camargo
São Paulo, January 1975

Contents

1 Historical development of mass communication in Brazil

Taking as a principle that communication is the set of human interactions and their means of expression through the use of techniques, considered both in time and space, we can follow the evolution of mass communication, in Brazil, practically from the moment of the integration of the American continent into the European cultural complex.

The discovery of Brazil (1500) is a chapter of European geographic expansion (fifteenth and sixteenth centuries), especially Portugal's. It is different from the Spanish expansion which, in America, entered in contact with highly sophisticated cultures such as those of the Aztecs and Incas. The Portuguese in Brazil found nomad cultures, with very primitive characteristics.

This is an important ingredient in understanding the cultural fusion and communication processes between the Portuguese and indigenous population.

Mimicry was the first communication system; Pero Vaz de Caminha, Brazil's first European chronicler, wrote in 1500 that music and dance were much appreciated. Writing about a Portuguese sailor with a bagpipe, he says that he 'introduced himself among them [the population] dancing, taking them by the hands and they were happy and laughed and followed him very gladly with the sound of the pipe; after dancing, he jumped fast and again jumped, so they were astonished and laughed and enjoyed it very much'.

This first contact between Portuguese and natives was characterized by a cordiality which would remain for some years. The tropics' attraction, the shipwrecks and the sensuality that characterized the European–native relationships, were the main constant forces present throughout the beginning of Brazilian colonization.

Two castaways of this period had great importance for their services to colonization: for example João Ramalho and Diogo Alvares Correia lived in harmony among Indian tribes, learned their languages and had numerous children. They acted as a communication tool between the European and the native culture; they were the first interpreters and their children formed the first mixed generation. The first generation was also bilingual, learning both Portuguese from their fathers and the native language from their mothers. Language was initiating its communication function in the new land.

The picture started changing by 1532, when Portugal decided to implant an economic and administrative system in its American colony. Brazil was divided into 'hereditary captainships' and the sugar-plantation system needed a labour-force that only natives could offer. The cultural shock was immediate the moment the European tried to enslave the natives, forcing them into agrarian labour. As in many primitive cultures, the working diversification pattern among the Brazilian tribes was related to sex: to men went the tasks of war, fishing and hunting; to women, agriculture. To ask a native man to work the earth, to plant and to harvest was to offend him deeply. The Indians did not submit.

There were fights which caused the destruction of various colonial nuclei; the metropolitan government was forced to take new measures: a centralized government was instituted in Salvador (formerly Bahia, in the north east) by 1548, and slaves were imported from Africa to work on the sugar plantations.

With the new general government, the first Jesuits came to Brazil nine years after the creation of Loyola's Company of Jesus. They came to teach and convert within the spirit of the new order.

Their efforts started by the learning of native language, as Priest Manoel da Nõbrega testified: 'We have been working to learn the language and Priest Navarro does better than anyone of us. We are determined to live with them, as we feel more confortable and sure, learning the language with them and indoctrining them.'

After their learning phase, the Jesuits started teaching the Christian doctrine to the native children. Nõbrega writes: 'Brother Vicente Rijo teaches the doctrine to the children everyday and also maintains the school for reading and writing; this seems to me a good way of bringing into the fold the natives of this land, who have a great wish to learn, and when asked if they so want, they show great enthusiasm.'

The next phase was the building of high schools and applied pedagogy. Besides reading and writing, they used music, dance and theatre as means of communication. Writing to Rome, Nõbrega (1552) considered it correct to let the 'Indians' remain with some of their habits 'neither opposed to Catholic faith, nor dedicated to idols, such as singing our Lord's songs in their own language, in its own tune and playing their musical instruments'.

With singing and playing, dancing was encouraged as 'a means of education, entertainment and art'.

Theatre was another communication vehicle of the period. As in the church in the European Middle Ages, the Jesuits used it to attract and persuade new disciples about the validity of Christian principles through simple and didactic plays.

Popular theatres were built to show the *autos*: the *St. James*, *The Universal Sermon* or *St. Lawrence* were played in Portuguese and native languages in order to be understood by everybody.

At the same time, the Jesuits aimed at the preservation and cultivation of European cultural patterns in Brazil. The *Colégios* (high schools) founded in Salvador and São Paulo were the roots of the Brazilian élite.

The seventeenth and eighteenth centuries mark the expansion of sugar culture, with the growing of an agrarian aristocracy supported by the latifundia and the enslaved labour of the African negro. In the sugar civilization, the principal institution is the sugar-mill, characterized by the 'Great house', where the all-powerful 'master', head of a patriarchal clan, was the main figure.

In the sugar-mill there coexisted a capitalist system of sugar exportation and a self-supply system of goods for consumption, similar, in this aspect, to the European Middle Ages feudal system. This system of colonization, because of the sugar-mill isolation, did not favour the emergence of the urbanization processes, with their more dynamic processes of communication.

Of the Brazilian cities of the eighteenth century, only three had urban characteristics: Salvador, Recife and Rio de Janeiro. As commercial harbours, they grew by exchanging Portuguese and local products. Salvador, the base of the central administration, was the most important city, due to the presence of the governor-general (later viceroy) and the colonial administrative and judiciary power. A commercial bourgeoisie lived in Salvador, Recife and Rio de Janeiro. It was responsible for the import of European goods and their distribution in the country.

Within this system, ships and mule trains became means of communication. The fleets were composed by numerous ships that linked Europe and Brazil. The official and private correspondence, the oral reports, the news and features were conveyed through them.

The mule trains transported goods and foods received from overseas from the ports to the hinterland.

Reflecting the European economy—on which it depended for its sugar exports—the Brazilian economy suffered a hard crisis in the second half of the seventeenth century. That fact brought on the fever of precious-metals exploration, as a means to solve the crisis. Many stories about the fabulous silver mines of Peru circulated at the time, stimulating the Portuguese-Brazilian imagination. Encouraged by the Portuguese Crown, expeditions left for the central part of Brazil, the middle-west, and discovered the gold mines of the present-day states of Minas Gerais (General Mines), Goiás, Mato Grosso and Bahia, during the late eighteenth and early nineteenth centuries.

Deep transformation in the evolution of Brazil follows this. The miners did not grow crops: the mining centres were dependent upon the other areas for provisions. The new wealth created truly continent-wide trails and produced the need of a continental inter-communication system. Between 1704 and 1707 a 'New Way' to link Rio de Janeiro and Minas Gerais was opened; this is the starting-point of Rio's opulence as the great gold *entrepôt*. Between 1736 and 1737, the large road that linked the Mato Grosso region to the mines of Goiás was completed, opening the way to the São Francisco Valley. Salvador, the end of this line, changed from a port of sugar into a port of gold, vying with Rio de Janeiro for the commerce of the mines.

By 1749, the link was completed through the Tapajós River, between the Mato Grosso mines and Belém do Pará. The link with the Amazon, through the Guaporé and Madeira rivers completed the set.

During the eighteenth century other structural changes occurred in many sectors of Brazilian life, besides the communication complex. Demographic growth increased. Immigrants from Portugal and other nations filled the ships (Portugal tried to stop it with no result); from many parts of Brazil, populations moved in the direction of the mines.

Antonil, a contemporary chronicler, portrays the flow of people, writing that 'each year lots of Portuguese and other foreigners come by ship to seek the way to the mines. From the cities, villages, farms and remote lairs come the whites, "half-castes" and negroes, and many natives who work for the Paulistas. [1] The blend is made of men and women, old and young, poor and rich, noble and common, secular, clergy and religious people.'

The Brazilian population estimated as 300,000 inhabitants by 1700, was estimated around 3 million by 1800, that is, a growth of 1,000 per cent.

Another important transformation took place in the urban sector. Besides Rio de Janeiro and Salvador, originating from the sugar economy, the mining region become, as a whole, the most important urbanized part of Brazil. In a few decades the miners' poor camps changed into villages and, not long after, to opulent cities. In these cities, during this period, flourished the Brazilian baroque, as an artistic expression of the Brazilian golden age.

Differently from the agrarian economy based on sugar—where the city was an extension of the sugar-mill—the mining economy stimulated urban life. The lord–slave dichotomy, characteristic of the sugar era, broke with the emergence of an urban middle class formed by liberal professionals and free workers. Medical doctors and lawyers became the new élite; teachers, merchants, musicians, artists and public officers were detached from the mass of slaves. For the first time in Brazilian history, the city acquired personality and started performing by the end of the eighteenth century as a centre of decisions and a radiating point of new ideas.

At this moment, Brazil was affected by the North Atlantic revolutionary waves: the American Revolution, the French Revolution and the Industrial Revolution. Through the ways opened by commerce, the ideas started being discussed and the Brazilian élite became conscious of the tensions of the colonial system. Books, newspapers and ideas, even though prohibited by Portuguese censorship, circulated via secret societies (Freemasonry); little by little, movements against the colonial isolationist monopoly grew: the Inconfidência Mineira (1789), the Rio de Janeiro Rebellion (1794), the Inconfidência Baiana (1797) and the Revolução Pernambucana (1817) are typical examples.

The Inconfidência Baiana of 1797 shows the role of the means of communication. As the metropolitan censorship prohibited any publications in Brazil, revolutionary groups utilized clandestine pamphlets affixed at public places. The first pamphlet appeared on 12 October 1797, and shows the circulation of the French Revolution ideals: liberty, equality, fraternity:

---

1. Inhabitants of the province of São Paulo, famous as pioneers who discovered the mines and enlarged the Brazilian territory to almost its present boundaries.

'Cheer up, Bahiense people, the happy moment of our liberty is near; the time when all will be brothers; the time when all will be equal.'

A totally unexpected fact modified completely the political situation of the colony. As a consequence of Napoleonic expansion and the invasion of Portugal by the French army, the Portuguese royal family left for Brazil (1808) bringing along the entire Portuguese imperial administration.

The Portuguese king's decree 'opening Brazilian harbours to all friendly nations' was the first rupture of the Brazilian colonial system. Isolation was broken: British and American ships (the only two nations friendly to the Portuguese during the Napoleonic age) started calling on Brazilian harbours; then, after Napoleon's defeat, flags, news and information from the whole world entered through Brazilian ports.

The second step of the rupture was the press and printing permit, which had been forbidden and strongly repressed long since Brazil's discovery. With official permission the first Brazilian newspaper was printed on 10 September 1808. It was named *A Gazeta do Rio de Janeiro* and was published on a printing machine brought over by the Portuguese Minister of War, Don Altino de Araujo, in his flight from Napoleon's armies. As an official gazette, it informed its public solely of the health of the reigning houses of Europe, public notices, birthdays, obituaries of the court and praise for the king and his family. At about the same time, however, Hipólito da Costa, a Brazilian expatriate in London, started publication of the *Correio Braziliense*, the first opinion periodical in Brazil. It was a monthly newspaper with over a hundred pages. Its circulation in Brazil was clandestine, smuggled in by ships coming from England. Press and printing in Brazil had characteristics quite different from other Latin American countries. In Spanish America the press was precocious: in 1533 it appeared in Mexico and in 1584 in Lima (Peru). In English-speaking America, the first printing machine dates from 1638. The first newspaper printed in the United States was in 1960; the first in Spanish America, in 1722 in Mexico. In Brazil, the transference of the Portuguese court was necessary to permit the existence of the press and printing machines as means of communication.

Newspaper expansion was slow. Rio de Janeiro (1808) was the first region with a periodical; the Amazon (1852) was the last Brazilian province to set up its press and print.

Censorship immediately followed (24 June 1808) the press installation in Brazil (18 May 1808). The Minister of the Interior was in charge of preventing any publications against religion, government and good manners. In September 1808, the first royal controllers were designated.

The seat of Portuguese government in Rio caused deep political changes: the colony status was raised to a Kingdom (1815); after the queen's death, the regent was crowned in Rio's cathedral (1818). These facts were politically important: first, while Spanish America declared its independence under the influence of the French and American Revolutions, in Brazil a monarchy was being implanted; second, the transfer of the Portuguese treasury to Rio and the great commercial incentive provoked by the 'opening of the harbours', favoured by the conflicts in the Atlantic, stimulated a real boom in socio-economic life, due, undoubtedly, to the presence of the court.

In Portugal, discontentment led to the Pôrto revolution (1820) which adopted the constitutional monarchy system and forced the king's return (1821). His eldest son remained as regent of the Brazilian kingdom; this fact is the starting-point of the Brazilian independence process.

The Portuguese *bourgeoisie* in power, in Portugal, could not tolerate the colony's new commercial freedom and the loss of its old privileges. The fight against the king was violent.

The Brazilian élite surrounded the regent and got him progressively involved with the independence cause: he disobeyed the Court's order to return to Portugal (January 1822), accepted the title of 'Perpetual Protector of Brazil' (May 1822) and finally convoked a Constitutional Assembly (June 1822). Independence was practically complete: the Portuguese Court's decrees annulling the regent's acts precipitated matters and forced the Independence Declaration on 7 September 1822. The 1824 Constitution declared the constitutional monarchy as the Brazilian system of government, which lasted until 1899.

The press acted during this process as a real mass medium of communication. Freed from censorship in 1821, it became the instrument to circulate the ideals of the Brazilian élite, and oriented the urban masses. From this moment on it became definitely attached to Brazilian political movements.

Brazilian independence came at an unfavourable economic conjuncture. The world's great recession of the nineteenth century had its consequence in Brazil, provoking an economic and political crisis which led the first emperor to abdicate (1831). Here, too, the role of the press was decisive.

After the abdication, since the heir was a child, a regent had to take over the government and face continuous revolutions all over the country, which, if victorious, would have led to the geographic fragmentation of Brazil. Finally, the prince was declared emperor, at the age of 14. At this time an astonishing number of newspapers and pamphlets were already being published all over Brazil. In 1827 there were twelve but in 1831 there were fifty-four periodical newspapers—sixteen in the capital. Most of these papers were short-lived, publishing up to six or eight issues. But those which disappeared were quickly replaced by new ones.

The emperor's long administration was a period of prosperity and great technical change, thanks to the coffee culture. Well adapted in the south-western part of the country, mainly in São Paulo, favoured by the world demand and reaching high market prices, coffee became the main export product. Brazilian external commerce reached a favourable level during the second half of the nineteenth century.

Population increase was significant. From 3 million (1800) to 17,318,556 inhabitants (1900). The important fact was the demographic inversion between the northern and southern part of the country. In the 1890 census, the south and south-east together, for the first time, had a larger population than the north and north-east, thus reflecting the displacement of the economic axis from the decadent north-east sugar economy to the booming coffee economy. New cities developed as strategic points of coffee culture: São Paulo, Santos, Campinas.

Nineteenth-century communications developed in Brazil in this context. Twenty-four years after the appearance of the first railway in England, the railway between Rio and Petrópolis was inaugurated (1845); collective transport was implanted in Rio; navigation increased on the River Amazon; the first submarine cable was inaugurated by the emperor (1874) with a message to Pope Pius IX, to Queen Victoria of England and other European heads of state. The expansion of the telegraphic system was great, mainly in the south, due to the war against Paraguay. The postal service was modernized (Brazil was the second country to utilize stamps as a tariff for postal services). At this period, the Brazilian telephone network began being laid out.

All these technical innovations helped the press to become an important vehicle of mass communication. The great obstacle for the quantitative growth of the press was illiteracy, in spite of the government's efforts to make elementary education compulsory and to build elementary schools in all provinces.

After the first turbulent years of independence, when censorship was constantly exerted, relative freedom during the second empire allowed the growth and stabilization of the Brazilian press. During this period, press specialization reflects social complexity and diversification. Periodicals on law, medicine, dentistry, economy, music, theatre, literatur and so forth, appeared together with newspapers printed in foreign languages (German, English, French, Italian and Spanish) to meet the immigrants' demand. The birth of a labour press marks the growth of the industrial working class and of the industrialization process. But the 'great press' remained a political press, characterized during this period by the campaign against slavery.

By moving public opinion against slavery, attacking the slavocrats, playing on the aggressions and tortures inflicted on slaves, the Brazilian press led the movement that, on 13 May 1888, abolished slavery in Brazil.

During the nineteenth century, journalism and literature marched side by side and this has greatly contributed to the 'mass' characteristic of the Brazilian press and to its public acceptance. In Brazil, as well as in Europe at the same period, the publication of fascicles became fashionable. Great Brazilian novelists had their books edited in weekly chapters (very much as radio and television soap operas do today). Within an almost illiterate population the fascicle created *soirées*, in which stories were read in a loud voice while the listeners were thrilled by it. [1]

1. Manuel Antonio de Almeida, José de Alencar, Machado de Assis, Joaquim Manuel de Macedo and Raoul Pompéia are some of the major authors of this period of Brazilian literature, considered even today among the best.

The success of this kind of reading led the Brazilian entrepreneurs to buy foreign novels, mainly French ones. However, by the end of the nineteenth and the begining of the twentieth century Brazilian literature was practically out of the market, substituted in many cases by melodramatic novels that had nothing to do with Brazilian reality. From this moment on one can follow the track of foreign 'canned' material in the Brazilian mass media.

Politically, the end of the nineteenth century in Brazil was marked by the growth of the republican ideal. By 1870 the *A República* (The Republic) newspaper appeared; in the same year *The Republican Manifesto* was published. This fact is very significant regarding the freedom of the press, since it shows the open propaganda of the republic within a monarchic system. In this environment of freedom, the republican press boomed as a vehicle of indoctrination and campaign against monarchy.

The press in 1889 is thus described by Max Leclerc, a French journalist who was visiting Brazil at the time:

On one side there are some very prosperous large newspapers, with a powerful material organization depending mainly on advertising; therefore organized above all as a business enterprise, with the intention of extending the circle of their readers to increase the value of its publicity rather than exerting influence in orienting public opinion. These newspapers show a certain independence, a certain mocking scepticism, or show impartiality. . . . On the other a multicolour multitude of party papers exist which, far from being profitable, make a living from party subsidies, groups or individual politicians and are only read if the man who backs them is in evidence or is feared.

A military *coup d'état* an 15 November 1889 changed the system of government from monarchical to republican.

The first republican years coincide with end of the nineteenth century and with one of the most exuberant periods of world history. In Europe and in the United States the period is characterized by deep and violent changes caused by the technical revolution and the growth of industrialization. Distant world regions are linked by telegraph; the telephone facilitates human contacts; the first cinematographic experiments succeed; the press becomes a capitalist enterprise; propaganda starts stimulating consumption; the first cars appear, changing urban structures; finally, man starts the long adventure of flight conquest, with the dirigibles and the first planes.

Unfortunately for Brazil, this period emphasizes the backwardness in its development in comparison to the vertiginous growth of industrialized nations such as England, Germany and the United States. The political crisis of the first republican years, the emphasis on the coffee monoculture and its absolute predominance as the country's main export product limited the development of transportation to the railways and roads, concentrated mostly in the south, as a function of the coffee economy.

A change in the world scene was necessary to provoke alterations in the

Brazilian socio-economic structure. The inflexibility of coffee prices, in spite of the increasing world production, brought the first crisis to the Brazilian basic export product. From 1906 to 1929, this crisis was practically continuous, mostly during the socio-economically disturbed decade of the 1920s.

The First World War was the second factor of the Brazilian republic socio-economic change. Its effects, plus the coffee crisis, caused the acceleration of the industrializing process of the country and changed drastically the urban scene, mostly in São Paulo.

The social and political inquietude of this period, allied to the devasting effects of the 1929 crisis, led to a revolution (1930) aimed to overthrow the coffee oligarchy. Getúlio Vargas, its leader, little by little spread his personal power. With a *coup d'état* in 1937 he established a dictatorial régime in Brazil and used the radio largely as a tool for his political purposes.

Officially, radio was introduced in Brazil during the Independence Centennial Commemoration Fair in Rio de Janeiro in 1922. The opening address of the fair by the president of the republic was transmitted to Niteroi, São Paulo and Petrópolis simultaneously, thanks to the transmission and reception service set up by the Rio de Janeiro and São Paulo Telephone Company and the Western Electric Company.

Radio expansion was slow, mainly due to equipment costs and the difficulties created by the government to buy and use sets. Nevertheless, between 1923 and 1940 almost all state capitals and main cities had at least one transmitter station.

The contemporaneity of radio expansion and Getúlio Vargas' political ascension, led to the use of radio as a medium of political propaganda. As Roosevelt, Hitler and Mussolini, Vargas knew how to use radio as a political communication tool, a great part of his charismatic power came from his direct appeal to the Brazilian people by radio, through his well-known opening line:—'Workers of Brazil . . .'—which electrified the Brazilian masses.

The Vargas period, as it could not be otherwise, was marked by strict mass media censorship. Information control in Brazil was regulated by federal decrees, by the 1937 Constitution, and was exerted by the Department of Press and Propaganda (DIP) created on 30 December 1939. Prior censorship covered everything: the press, the theatre, cinema, radio and editorial activities.

With the Second World War, the Vargas system faced contradictory forces. The Brazilian international compromises led the country to enter the war on the allied side. Brazilian expeditionary forces fought the European totalitarian systems of government. At the war's end, the country's discontent, the return of the Brazilian armed forces which fought for democracy in Europe, made the Brazilian internal contradiction evident, precipitating the fall of the dictatorship in November 1945.

The 1945 Constitution, elaborated in a moment of world euphoria, democratic faith and creation of the United Nations, reflected this spirit. The country enjoyed complete freedom of expression: the Brazilian

17

journalistic boom was characterized by reaction to the extinct censorship and by the diversification of political interests and specialities. The country's wealth grew during wartime, as the war strongly pushed foward its industrial development, speeded up the urbanization process and deeply changed the traditional agrarian structure of Brazil. The increase of electric power, the paving of roads, the introduction of new technologies made possible fast communications and full mass media utilization.

In spite of the electrical-power growth, not all Brazilian territory had electricity, many regions thus remained isolated from information sources. The radio transistor, introduced all over the country, brought about a true revolution in the country's communication situation, with important socio-cultural implications.

At the moment of radio-transistor development in Brazil, another medium was inaugurated: television. The first programme was broadcast on 18 September 1950 in São Paulo.

Television expansion in Brazil was slow at first, but steady. High costs of transmitters, reception sets, production and so forth, limited its diffusion during the first decade to the Rio–São Paulo axis. Today, television is the most important medium of mass communication, mainly in urban centres.

Associated to the industrial and mass media development, commercial propaganda grew fast, being an important enterprise sector in the country.

This period of growth and freedom (1945–60) has its peak in the inauguration of Brasília, the new capital of Brazil. The years immediatly following were characterized by interminable political crises and galloping inflation which led to the 1964 revolution.

After the 1964 revolution, important political, social and economic events took place. In 1967 the Ministry of Communications was created, reflecting the new government's interest in the role of communications in the development of modern Brazil.

Due to internal political conditions the government issued, in 1968, its Institutional Act No. 5 which considerably enlarged the scope of competence of federal legislation, suspending certain constitutional provisions.

During this period, considerable economic growth took place in the country: large programmes on housing, urban development and transportation changed Brazil substantially and allowed a constant increase of the Gross National Product (GNP). Exports increased fivefold from U.S.$1,400 million in 1964 to U.S.$7,300 million in 1974.

2 The system of mass communication within the socio-economic and cultural structures of the country

2.1 General considerations

From the outset one must bear in mind, when considering Brazil in its human aspects, the peculiar conditions created by its size. Its continental area (8,511,965 square kilometres) extends from latitude 5°16′ N, to 33°45′ S, with a distance of 4,320 km from north to south and over 7,800 km of sea coast. One can realize the country's dimension by considering that a trip from São Paulo to Pôrto Alegre, two southern cities, would equal a trip from Portugal to Denmark, going through Spain, France, Belgium and the Netherlands.

With over 105 million inhabitants the country may be divided into five main regions: northern, with 42 per cent of the total area and 4 million inhabitants; north-eastern, 18 per cent of the total area and 31 million inhabitants; south-eastern, 11 per cent of the total area and 44 million inhabitants; southern, 7 per cent of the total area and 20 million inhabitants; central-western, 22 per cent of the total area and 6 million inhabitants.

One of the difficulties encountered when trying to understand Brazil is due to attempts to deal with the country as a whole. Although the country succeeded in achieving a national character and some common traits throughout its territory, diversity in several fields, mainly cultural, prevail.

This situation has an important bearing in the development of communications in Brazil. It justifies the existence of highly complex communication systems in some areas of the country, while in others even the traditional press finds operational conditions very difficult. It also explains the role of electronic media (radio and television) in Brazil today.

2.2 Population growth, ethnic composition and education

The Brazilian population has been rapidly expanding as a result of the high natural growth index (62 births per 1,000 inhabitants). Increase in living standards and industrialization did not produce a drop of the birth rate in Brazil. The extension of medical and sanitary services and the improvement of hygienic and dietary habits are responsible for a large excess of births over deaths.

In general terms, one of the characteristics of the Brazilian population is its youth: 50 per cent of the population is under 20 years of age and 70 per cent under 30.

Urbanization has been a strong characteristic in the last few years. In 1950, 20 per cent of the population was urban, the remaining 80 per cent living in rural areas. Now, 60 per cent of the population live in cities, only 40 per cent remaining in rural areas. As a corollary to this tendency, the growth of cities of over 100,000 inhabitants has been remarkable. In 1940, only ten cities were above this figure: São Paulo, Rio de Janeiro, Recife, Salvador, Pôrto Alegre, Belo Horizonte, Belém, Santos, Fortaleza and Niteroi. In 1960, this figure grew to thirty-one cities. In 1974 it was over ninety and today its number is estimated at 140 cities.

Ethnically the Brazilian population indicates a frequent and diversified interrelationship among the three elements that contributed to its formation: whites, Negroes and Indians. These interrelationships occurred not only at the biological level but were also responsible for many of the socio-cultural characteristics of Brazil today.

Intermarriage on a large scale is to be found mostly in the northern and north-eastern regions but also exists in some areas of the south-eastern and central-western regions.

In these areas one can find the influence of the Negroes, whose contribution to the demographic composition of Brazil is due to their role in the colonial system, particularly in the economic areas outlined by the end of the eighteenth century. In other areas of the north and north-eastern regions, the Indian contribution was substantial. The southern states from São Paulo downwards, have a predominantly white racial composition, due to the heavy influence of European immigration.

As a natural result of the general evolution of the country, levels of education have improved considerably in the last few years. Illiteracy among those over 15 years of age in Brazil covered 56 per cent of the population in 1950, against less than 30 per cent in 1974.

Substantial increases in 1974, in comparison to 1964 were made: 40 per cent in primary-school enrolment; 350 per cent in secondary school and 300 per cent in university.

2.3 Economy

The Brazilian GNP has more than doubled in the last ten years, to its present level of 80,000 million dollars. The continual yearly increases at levels above 9 per cent for the last seven years have allowed *per capita* income to go from $312 in 1964 to $800 in 1974.

Once again one must avoid the pitfall of generalization. A breakdown of *per capita* income by regions will show quite a different picture from the over-all figure. The *per capita* income in the north-eastern region is roughly 50 per cent of the national average.

For historical reasons the south-eastern region is clearly the economic leader of the nation with 70 per cent of the Brazilian labour-force, and 75 per cent of its industrial production concentrated around the large metropolis of São Paulo and Rio de Janeiro.

The southern region is relatively rich, based on agriculture and industrialization of agricultural products.

The northern region, with a low *per capita* income, has been subject to a strong federal effort to improve its present level. A system of fiscal and financial incentives has been established in order to encourage Brazilian and foreign companies to invest in the area. However, it still has very serious problems and an adjustment of federal policies is now in course.

The Amazon region, the northern part of Brazil, is an enormous demographic void. The recent discoveries of iron ore, bauxite, nickel, coal, zinc, lead and copper, as well as some oil, have now encouraged the federal government into a policy of 'economic poles' based on mineral wealth as well as forest resources. The earth's biggest hydrological reserve (20 per cent of all the fresh water on the globe) is now being studied in order to set up hydro-electric plants. Cattle raising has also increased in the region.

Transportation has always been a very serious hindrance to the development of the region. Although it has a large river network, the free navigation all year through is possible in only a few rivers and for relatively short distances. For this reason, the federal government decided in 1972 to build a road system, criss-crossing the region.

Brazil is at present, in a depression-ridden world, still an oasis of economic boom. Although outside effects of the world situation will be increasingly felt, the country feels the boom will go on because of the following facts:
1. Basic exports will remain in high demand and at high price levels for the next few years (mainly alimentary products).
2. The domestic market is very far from being saturated in large sectors of products (cars, refrigerators, houses, clothing, foods, industrial equipment, transportation, etc).
3. The country will not be dependent on oil imports for its development, due to huge oil discoveries which will make it self-supporting in the near future.

2.4 Political system

Brazil is a republic composed of twenty-two states, a federal district and four territories. The federal government functions under a classic three-power system: the executive, run by the president and his ministers, the legislative, with the House and the Senate, and the judiciary, with the Supreme Court.

The executive branch, formerly elected by direct vote, is now chosen by an electoral college composed of all deputies and senators plus a proportional representation of each of the states' assemblies. The president runs the executive through his ministers, appointed and freely dismissible by him. Besides the ministers, the executive branch has several institutions in the fields of finance, housing, transportation, tourism, etc., but each one is under the operational control of the ministry to which its field of activity refers.

The legislative branch is composed of the House (proportional representation) and the Senate (three senators per state)—all elected by direct vote. Brazil lives under a two-party system. In the recent elections (1974) for the House and the Senate, the party at present in government (ARENA) returned 204 deputies and won six of the twenty-two senate seats at stake. The opposition party (MDB) won 160 seats in the House and won the remaining sixteen Senate seats at stake.

The Supreme Court is composed of justices appointed by the executive branch with the approval of the legislative branch.

The states have a considerable degree of autonomy, running their own legislation on court procedure, education, transportation, food supplies, police, health and finances.

Each state has a governor, elected by the state assembly. Deputies are elected every five years by direct vote. ARENA controls the majority of the state assemblies with the important exceptions of the states of São Paulo, Rio de Janeiro and Rio Grande do Sul.

Each state is subdivided into municipalities, each with its elected mayor and the elected council of aldermen. There are nearly 4,000 municipalities in Brazil.

The relative autonomy of each of the political subdivisions of Brazil is mainly due to the distribution of the tax system which allows sufficient means for accomplishing respective goals. The federal government collects income tax, custom duties, industrialized goods tax and oil derivate tax. The states collect sales tax, and the municipalities property taxes with a participation of 20 per cent of sales tax collected in its territory. The federal government functions as a re-distributor of wealth, investing in the poorer states the taxes collected in the richer regions.

3 Public policy

3.1 Legislation

Brazilian communication legislation has not been subject to any uniform codification. Therefore, there are many laws about the subject, the main ones being: the law of national security, the law of press and the national code of telecommunications. Special decrees regulate cinematographic activities, the theatre and public entertainment. Recommendations and suggestions by boards of censors complete the actual government–mass media interaction.

Mass media is basically a private enterprise in Brazil. Being such a large country, government historically invested in those areas where private investments do not exist, providing the infrastructure for later investments. In the case of the mass media, the Brazilian system works on the basis of private investment and government supervision. The government does not operate but supervises mass media performances.

Brazilian legislation very often covers under the same law matters pertaining to content of mass communication as well as matters regarding authorization, organization and functioning of mass communication enterprises. Therefore, it is easier to deal with the matter as a whole by grouping the legal texts.

In this chapter we shall analyse the contents of the Brazilian law on information, the National Code of Telecommunications, cinema legislation and censorship legislation.

3.1.1 The Brazilian law on information

Although the law is officially named 'Press Law' it refers in a much broader sense to information as a whole. It deals not only with the press in the strict sense, but also comprises norms regarding radio, television and news agencies.

The law is divided into seven chapters, the first dealing with liberty of thought and expression, the second with registration of mass communication enterprises, the third with abuses of freedom of expression, the fourth with the right of response, the fifth with criminal procedures and responsibilities, the sixth with civil responsibility and the seventh with general provisions of the law.

3.1.1.1. *Freedom of thought*

The Brazilian law on information explicitly recognizes freedom of thought through expression, searching, reception and diffusion of information without prior censorship,[1] as every one is responsible, by the law, for the abuses committed. It is also explicit that propaganda of war, political or social subversion and race or class prejudice will not be tolerated.

Censorship is not exerted on the publication and circulation over the national territory of books, newspapers and other periodicals, if legally registered, except when offensive to morals and social customs. The same is true for foreign publications, the exception being those which offend the articles stated by law (internal and external security, distorted facts which provoke social alarm or disturb public order, mistrust or credit rupture of the banking system, enterprises, or private individuals, damage to the credit of the union, states, federal district or the counties, disturbances on commodity and stock markets).

To sell, display for sale or distribute such materials is subject to fines and seizure. In the case of offence to public morals, immediate seizure can be ordered to avoid circulation.

In all cases of restriction or seizure, judicial recourse is guaranteed. Therefore, whenever a court does not maintain the act of the government agent, the union or the state must compensate for damages and losses.

3.1.1.2 *Ownership*

The ownership of mass media enterprises, whether political or simply informative, is reserved only for Brazilians. Foreign nationals and corporations or any juridical entities—except the national political parties—cannot be partners or stockholders in the ownership of journalistic and other mass media enterprises, nor exert any type of direct or indirect control over them.

The administrative and intellectual orientation and responsibility for mass media enterprises is reserved for Brazilians. By definition, a mass media enterprise is any corporation that publishes newspapers, magazines and other periodicals, or operates radio or television stations or news agencies.

Scientific, technical and artistic publications, however, are not subject to this rule.

Any technical or hardware supply contract of radio and television enterprises with foreign organizations are subject to approval by the National Council of Telecommunications (CONTEL). The law forbids any contractual arrangement with foreign enterprises which imply the right of direct or indirect participation on the profits of Brazilian mass media enterprises.

---

1. By law, censorship may be exerted over the mass media and news agencies by the government during a period of siege, on matters related to motives of the siege and by the persons legally authorized to exert it. The motives that can determine the siege are specified by the 1967 Constitution (Article 152). Censorship is also exerted upon public shows and entertainment. A law of 1970 (No. 1077, January) establishes censorship in matters of ethical and moral patterns for national or foreign publications and shows, which are to be submitted to the Ministry of Justice.

3.1.1.3 *Abuses*

A number of abuses have criminal sanctions. The law, however, allows the right of criticism. The journalist does not commit an infraction while examining via the press the public life of a candidate to an elective position 'since it is a journalist's right and duty in the relevant mission of the press in democratic countries, to prepare citizens for the exercise of voting'.[1]

Brazilian jurisprudence is rich in precedents about the just measure of the right to inform and the right to privacy. The Brazilian law on information leaves opportunity for the judge's interpretation.

3.1.1.4 *Civil responsibilities*

Besides the penal action, the law defines the civil responsibility by which the person, who in the exercise of the freedom of expression of thought and information, violates rights or causes harm to any one is obliged to compensate the moral and material damages.

3.1.1.5 *Anonymity*

In the free manifestation of thought, anonymity in not permitted; but the sources of information are protected.

3.1.2 *The National Code of Telecommunications*

Law No. 4117 of 1962 creates a National Council of Telecommunications (CONTEL) composed of the heads of the federal agencies in charge of the post, telegraph and telex systems, of representatives of the Ministries of the Interior, Education, Foreign Affairs, Industry and Trade, and Defence (army, navy, air force).

CONTEL, as a regulatory body, supervises the activities of government-granted concessions, issues authorizations and permits for the use of telecommunications services and applies penalties.

Although private institutions may, according to regulations, operate radio and television stations, such services exist as a concession of the union which reserves for itself, by law, all powers regarding the ultimate use of radio and television. Therefore, any corporation which operates radio and television is actually enjoying a temporary and particular permit.

The federal government remains the ultimate legal proprietor of radio and television services. The heavy preponderance of public interest over radio—and television—station operators allows the federal government to modify, whenever justifiable, regulations and by-laws as well as the individual terms of concession.

The Code of Telecommunications also regulates matters regarding the execution of telecommunication services.

According to this law, directors and managers of concessionaire enterprises must be Brazilians; so must technicians in charge of the transmitters.

---

1. Freitas Nobre, *The Law of Information.*

Exceptionally CONTEL may agree to the admission of foreigners, if they are residents in the country, but for a limited time only. CONTEL supervises the subordination of the information, entertainment and propaganda radio and television services to educational and cultural goals; it obliges radio stations to transmit daily the *Hour of Brazil*, a government broadcast by the Agencia Nacional; it prohibits the participation of one single person in more than one board of directors of broadcasting companies in one city; it obligates television stations to devote at least 5 per cent their transmission time to news; it prohibits those people who enjoy parliamentary immunities from participating as directors or managers of radio and television concessionary enterprises.

To prevent erratic growth of radio and television networks, the code establishes radio-station limits. The number of local radio stations is limited to 4 broadcasting on medium wave bands and 6 on FM; regional radio stations to 3 on medium wave bands and 3 on tropical wave bands; and national radio to 2 on medium wave bands and 2 on short wave bands. The number of television stations is limited to 10 throughout the national territory.

The law requires that all transmissions must be tape recorded and preserved for twenty-four hours. Television stations may tape record only the sound of their programmes for such purposes. The text of all programmes, including news, must be preserved for sixty days; political programmes, debates, interviews, statements for twenty days.

Ninety days before general elections in the country, all radio and television stations must set aside two hours of unpaid time for political programming: one during the day and the second between 8 p.m. and 11 p.m. A rigorous criteria giving time to all political parties must be observed, in proportion to the number of representatives of each party in the national congress and legislative houses. The electoral justice is in charge of co-ordination of these arrangements. Political propaganda or the transmission of favourable or unfavourable ideas about any political party are forbidden outside the above-mentioned procedure.

3.1.3 *Cinema legislation*

The National Institute of Cinema (INC) is a federal organization under the Ministry of Education and Culture. It was created in 1966, by Law-decree No. 43, to formulate and implement the governmental policy related to the development of the Brazilian film industry, to its cultural improvement and its promotion outside the country.

The institute's responsibilities include regulating Brazilian film production, distribution and showings; price control; conditions of film import; proportion of compulsory showing of national films; archives and statistics; production and buying of educational films; co-production conditions; promotion of festivals, and related matters.

The law defines a Brazilian film as one which is produced by a Brazilian company in Portuguese, directed or cinematographically adapted by a Brazilian or by a resident (for more than five years) in the country; two-thirds of its technical and artistic cast must be Brazilians (or two-year residents); be shot on national territory (exceptions are permitted only in terms of fidelity to the plot); audio and mixing must be recorded in Brazil; negatives and copies for showing in the national territory must be developed and copied in Brazilian laboratories.

When utilizing a script based on Brazilian history, literature or culture, the director may be a foreigner if assisted by a Brazilian co-director. The INC is the judge of such projects.

The producer of cinematographic news-reels is obliged by law to insert at the begining of each film a film classified of educational interest, with no less than two minutes of showing. Such films are produced or acquired by the INC which distributes them at no cost to the producers of news-release films.

The censorship of cinematographic films is in the competence of the federal government. Films are judged in the federal district and released subject to age control.

One of the most important policies of the INC was the institution of the 'uniform cinema ticket', a numbered ticket issued by the INC, and which cinemas all over Brazil must use to deliver to the public as their admittance ticket after payment of the fee. This permits the INC to control in detail the sales of seats per cinema, per show, and establish the basis for calculation of royalties, subsidies, etc. It permits the INC to collect the copyright for music and phonograms included in films and played in the auditorium during the intermission.

3.1.4 *Censorship*

'To protect ethical values and assure the dignified and healthy formulation of youth', the Brazilian Constitution forbids any publications or demonstrations against accepted morality. 'Since there may be books and magazines which publish abscenities and TV channels which show programmes menacing the moral values of Brazilian society' [1] the law subjects any publications, public entertainment shows, as well as television and radio programmes, to previous examination.

The liberation of such material is up to the federal police which is given by law twenty days (for books) or forty-eight hours (for periodicals) to decide about its content. This measure does not apply to publications on philosophical, scientific, technical or didactic subjects which are exempt from previous verification.

Publications only for adults must be conveniently wrapped and sealed when sold at the news-stands or shops, covered by a visible belt with the

1. Consideranda of Decree-law No. 1077, 26 January 1970.

inscription 'Forbidden for those under 18 years of age'. Pornographic material is not permitted.

Adults who facilitate the access of youngsters to 'only-for-adults' material are subject to prosecution.

3.2 Planning

Until very recently, Brazil did not have a national communication plan. Its starting-point was the telecommunication plan, in 1962, with the creation of the National Council of Telecommunications (CONTEL), the National Fund of Telecommunications, the National Department of Telecommunications (DENTEL, 1965) and the Brazilian Telecommunications Enterprise (EMBRATEL).

In 1967, the Ministry of Communications was founded to facilitate communication centralization so that the national system of communications remains under government supervision, concessions being given for the services considered more efficient if run by private enterprises.[1]

Federal policy aims at stimulating the elaboration of regional plans in the states, integrated with the national plan, in order to avoid the multiplication of small companies operating with non-standardized equipment. These have in the past caused operational costs higher than necessary and many other problems of a technical, financial and organizational nature.

3.2.1 *The Brazilian Telecommunications Enterprise (EMBRATEL)*

EMBRATEL was founded to set up the basic operational net of the national system of telecommunications. In its four years of existence, it has completed the national micro-waves system (11,500 km net viability, 5,100 km Tropo-diffussion) linking main communication centres and establishing automatic long-distance telephone communication between a large number of Brazilian cities.

EMBRATEL is responsible for the national telex network: telegraphy, facsimile transmission of radio-photos for the journalistic enterprises and for the universities, data processing centres and terminals, high-fidelity radio transmissions, live transmissions of national and international television programmes (colour included) and the Brazilian participation in the International System of Communication.

Brazil has been member of the International Telecommunications Satellite Organization (INTELSAT) since 1969. [2]

1. It is a communication policy to review all radio and television concessions in order to overcome technical deficiencies and to avoid bankruptcies in communications enterprises, as well as to nationalize the use of power and wavelengths (Resolution 33 of 27 April 1973).
2. 1,200 voice channels and 1 with simultaneous television; 60 telephone channels for Europe; 96 channels for Latin American, North America and Africa.

Financial resources for EMBRATEL come from the national tele-communications fund, constituted by the telecommunication taxes on services such as the telephone, operated by the government-owned Brazilian Telephonic Company (CTB), television transmissions for the generating television commercial stations and interstate telephone operations. [1]

Parallel to the EMBRATEL basic system, the national system of telecommunications includes a complementary system constituted by nets of small capacity linking the cities in the interior of the country with the main system and a projected auxiliary system, low-capacity a network to link Brasília and Rio directly to the other capitals, as well as linking the centres with difficult access to the basic system as an emergency alternative. [2]

3.2.2 *Public versus private ownership*

A study of Brazilian laws and codes from 1931 to 1967 for telecommunications shows a long debate between private enterprise and the government, which still continues.

Private enterprise has tried to emphasize personal responsibility and freedom to run telecommunications as a business enterprise; the government has attempted to rule it as a public service, subject to government decisions.

From this controversy has emerged, in November 1962, the Brazilian Association of Radio and Television Enterprises, with regional and international connexions.

The ruling telecommunications code passed by the government in 1962 and modified by several federal laws in 1967, does not seem to be satisfactory either for the mass media enterprises, or for the government. As the congresses and seminars on the matter, many recommendations have been made on the procedures for radio and television in order to modify and adjust the legal requirements to concrete situations.

In the middle of 1974, the Ministry of Communications submitted to the federal congress a new and more refined code project, elaborated with the aid of the Brazilian Association of Radio and Television Enterprises. This project outlines a definition of objectives and a philosophy for communication through mass media.

The new code covers these problems as well as those that refer to the use of communication satellites, since there are plans to utilize them for education and public services; it defines a policy for the use of mass media for development and orientates sectorial policies; it encompasses, in a comprehensive way, the many questions to be answered through the use of mass media for 'National Development, Integration and Security', which are the upper goals expressed by the government plan for the term 1974–78.

1. In its four years of activity EMBRATEL invested $150 million in 11,500 km of microwaves systems (194 repetition stations).
2. The complementary system is being mainly set by the concessionnaire enterprises at state level.

This is a long and complex process to work out, when one realizes that the world is already considering the use of a laser for communication, while in Brazil there is not yet agreement upon the use of Hertzian waves, the education/entertainment balance on television, and other software questions and requirements. Such is the quantity and complexity of the problems to be solved by the boom of communication technology in a country that must overcome underdevelopment at an accelerated rhythm.

3.2.3 *Hardware and content*

Under the 1967 code, still in force, television and radio services are to be educational and cultural, even in their informational and entertainment programmes. Their commercial use is permitted as long as it does not interfere or harm those interests and goals.

This is the main principle. We have already mentioned that radio and television must dedicate at least 5 per cent of their programme times to transmission of news. They must too dedicate at least five hours weekly to the transmission of educational programmes. Advertising is limited to fifteen minutes per hour of transmission. Of course not all stations have the high standards intended by the law.

Not all cities in the far north are reached by the programmes or broadcasts transmitted by the main stations; large areas receive foreign broadcasts more easily than the national ones. To remedy this state of affairs the government is trying to build more potent radio and television transmitters.

A national policy of communication that includes not only technical items but also those dealing with social and educational aspects is urgently needed. This is even more evident because the national plan of development mentions explicitly 'national integration' as one of the most important government goals for the next four years.

From 1964 on, the Ministry of Communications gave priority to the building of the basic infrastructure for the 'telecommunication integration' of the country; microwave circuits of high capacity, the national telex network and the telephone network. The earth station that integrates the International Telecommunications Satellite Organization links Brazil directly to the whole world.[1]

These new systems are formed by: the Rio–São Paulo system; the Rio–Brasília system; the north-eastern branch; the São Paulo–Uberaba system; the west branch; the Rio–Vitória branch; the Fortaleza–São Luis system; the Belém–Brasília system; the Belém–São Luis system; and the Amazonia system of Tropodiffussion.

This last system is very important from a national security point of view, not only due to the extension of the region, but mainly for its nature and topography.

1. Itaberaí is the second station in Latin America and the fourteenth in the world.

As far as radio broadcasting is concerned, it is government policy to recognize that 'isolation' (that is, ownership of only one radio or television station) in communication media (television and radio) is incompatible with high standards in programming. Television operational costs in Brazil are very high. Independent stations, especially those located out of Rio and São Paulo, can hardly balance their budget with only local advertising and find it impossible to generate their own live programmes. It is practically impossible to operate a national television network without the participation of two main publicity markets (São Paulo and Rio): 'Since media policy is understood in terms of costs [Brazilian produced programmes are much more expensive], the media must creatively work to reduce cost and at the same time to improve production patterns.' [1]

Besides the legal regulations on hardware, labour and administrative matters, the Brazilian Government has shown, lately, particular interest in mass media content. In this matter, government policy is known through the ministers' special recommendations to the media through public addresses and interviews published by the mass media.

The main lines of the government's view on mass media communications' content may be summed up at this point as follows:

Brazilian commercial TV is based on a philosophy of private enterprise but, because of its strength of penetration and persuasion, it cannot be treated as other mass media, i.e. the Press. Because of its specific nature it must be entrusted with a great deal of responsibility in respect to culture, education and national efforts for development. This can only become true if the right message reaches the right audience. Commercial experience and research data might provide useful cues for such an enterprise.[2]

One of the main problems pointed out by the government is the import and transmission of 'canned materials' and the 'cultural invasion'.

57% of a TV programme is imported and 43% is produced by Brazilian technicians. From this 43%, 34% is foreign material, edited by Brazilian stations. That means, for 109 hours of a one week programme, only 31 are genuinely Brazilian: the other 78 are imported . . . commercial TV imposes upon children and youth a kind of culture that has nothing to do with Brazilian culture. . . Instead of acting as a factor of creation and diffusion of Brazilian culture, TV is playing the role of a privileged medium of cultural import, and is denaturing Brazilian creativity.[3]

1. Communication Minister's address to the sixth Brazilian Tele-education Meeting, Belo Horizonte, October 1974.
2. ibid.
3. Quoted from Communications Minister Euclides Quandt de Oliveira, conference at the College of Social Communication 'Anhembi', as published by *O Estado de São Paulo* on 20 November 1974.

At the same time new television and radio station networks are being set up, by government permit, in the states of Rio, São Paulo, Rio Grande do Sul and Amazonas in order to avoid the information monopoly. The existent laws about the 'size' of networks are being re-examined.

In this same line of thinking the government is very concerned with the content and level of programmes but has consistently denied any intention to suppress or substitute private enterprise ownership in mass media matters.

Brazil has adopted the commercial TV solution, private enterprise. There is no sense changing this policy. It is the Government's task to set minimal standards of quality and to set the goals to be reached through mass media. It is also a Government task to supervise the reaching of such patterns and goals. Finally, it is a Government task to complement private initiative, when it cannot function or does not want to[1]

The government has frequently called the attention of mass media producers to the quality of their production, for the excesses made in the name of originality, creativity and so forth, but lately there has been an increased concern about the cultural role of mass media in the preservation of national values and cultural characteristics.

All broadcasts have educational content and people who make them should be conscious of that. Educational TV should be seen as one of the resources the teacher shall use or must use, but it is a complement or has to be complemented by person-to-person action in the class-room. . . .

Commercial TV should understand that it must help improve the cultural standards of the people by the adequate production of news broadcasts, debates, novels, music and so forth, but these broadcasts must evolve from the existing patterns in the direction of excellence

. . . the Media shall maintain the proposed objectives of broadcasts and operate towards these objectives in a compatible language for each type of audience . . . the media must avoid the excess of foreign broadcasts—even the so-called educational ones—because they produce cultural harm, by imposing upon the youngsters, patterns of behaviour which do not belong to our way of living and do not improve our cultural standards. . . .[2]

The government is none the less conscious of the positive role played by television, as an agent of national integration:

Even though some of the TV heroes and idols do not necessarily convey what we could call 'culture' or 'education', casts have emerged and made the TV programmes reach better standards; professional careers have been opened, writers and producers have turned their attention to Bazilian culture: folklore,

---

1. Communications Minister Euclides Quandt de Oliveira, op. cit.
2. ibid.

history, literature, art, living patterns, sense of humour and so forth. By doing so, TV can stimulate the audiences in the search of better information and entertainment standards.[1]

The government is in the process of organizing the RADIOBRAS, a system of State-owned radio stations that will offer alternatives to the audiences rather than simply competing with commercial stations.

This system will be directed by an interministerial body of representatives from the Ministry of Communications—which will be assigned managerial and technical tasks—and from the Ministry of Education—which will be responsible for the software and broadcast content. In order to meet this objective, higher standards and patterns of production will be reached as well as the standardization of the means of production.

Quoting Mexican President Echeverria, at the World Communication Congress, the Brazilian Minister of Communications stated:

I believe TV has contributed to the psychic rupture which is the characteristic of our Civilization; I think that before this giant TV screen, the individual is alone, isolated, passive. Culture is another thing. Culture is dialogue. Culture is the discovery of truth. Culture is not passivity, even though the technology of making and broadcasting programmes is tremendously imposing. What we need is a constructive reflection with a great deal of self-criticism, so that the media managers could really meditate about what culture is and what the human being is.[2]

To perform the tasks promoting Brazilian development 'the country must have a National Policy of Communication to which all available means (state or commercially owned) shall be oriented by common objectives and national goals'.[3]

3.2.4 *Educational and cultural radio and television*

The use of mass media for education in Brazil was started in 1923 by Roquette Pinto with the creation of the Radio Sociedade do Rio de Janeiro, a radio station with an essentially cultural and educational character. This became later the Radio MEC (Ministry of Education and Culture) which still exists today, playing a basic role in the field.

In 1937 the Serviço de Rádio Educativo (Educational Radio Service) was created in the Ministry of Education, marking the public interest in tele-education.

The growth of radio and television broadcasts, as well as educational cinema production, made evident to the federal government the need of a definite policy.

1. *O Estado de São Paulo*, 20 November 1974.
2. Minister's address to the sixth Brazilian Tele-education Meeting, Belo Horizonte, October 1974.
3. Ibid.

In 1965, the Ministry of Education requested that CONTEL reserve a number of television channels solely for educational purposes. In 1967 the Fundação Centro Brasileiro de TV Educativa (Central Brazilian Foundation for Educational TV) was created and, in the next year, the first educational television station was opened, TV-U-11 of the Federal University of Pernambuco. Soon after, the São Paulo cultural television station—Fundação Padre Anchieta—was started.

In 1972 the Ministry of Education decided to create a national agency in charge of the co-ordination of all tele-educational activities. By Decree 70.185 of 23 February 1972, PRONTEL (National Programme for Tele-education) was started.

In order to be able to optimize the use of available educational technology, PRONTEL must cope with certain situations, some of which are characteristic of the present level of development of the country, such as: the continental dimensions of the nation and its varied cultural heritage; the large contingent of illiterate and unskilled population; the lack of manpower in educational fields; considerable population growth; school stratification.

The role of PRONTEL is: (a) to co-ordinate, promote and integrate the use and development of existing educational techniques as well as those under research; (b) to elaborate programmes as defined by the Ministry of Education; (c) to form a national educational broadcasting network to attend to regional and national needs.

At the present stage, education through mass media in Brazil may be grouped under three subsystems:

First is the subsystem of the Ministry of Education and Culture. This subsystem is directly operated by PRONTEL and functions mainly through three agencies: the Central Brazilian Foundation for Educational TV, the Educational Radio Service, as well as the Educational Department of the National Institute of Cinema.

The Central Brazilian Foundation for Educational TV, located in Rio de Janeiro, has large studios and is a production centre for instructional and cultural television materials. As the Ministry of Education and Culture under the norms of the National Code of Telecommunications demands five hours per week of educational programmes from commercial television stations, the centre is to produce materials for stations all over Brazil. The centre is now at the final stages of mounting its own television station— Channel 2—which will operate in the Rio de Janeiro area.

The Educational Radio Service was created in 1937; in 1970 it launched its Project Minerva which is retransmitted daily through all Brazilian radio stations. Its objective is to complement regular teaching on elementary and high-school levels, to give supplementary courses, to promote out-of-school education and to broadcast cultural programmes on music, arts, folklore and literature. Such goals are aimed at reaching everyone who wishes further education—children, youngsters, adults. Besides open reception, it has a system of controlled reception in about 6,100 radio clubs all over the country. It maintains 605 supervisors and distributes graphic materials to follow up the radio courses (1,500,000 booklets in 1973).

The INC (National Institute of Cinema) produces and buys through its Educational Division, filmstrips, slides and motion pictures for educational or culture purposes. It also buys and distributes audio-visual equipment to schools.

A second subsystem is the public subsystem of tele-education. This subsystem is composed of radio and television stations which belong to the federal, state, or municipal governments in Brazil. Of these, the Fundação Padre Anchieta, in São Paulo, is the largest. It is dedicated to the production and transmission of non-commercial radio and television broadcasts. It has been maintained by the government of the state of São Paulo since 1967, with approximately 400 employees (excluding artistes, professors and temporary staff).

It is a centre for television and radio production; besides its own broadcasts, it feeds programmes to many television and radio stations throughout the country. Programmes on educational and cultural subjects are produced in three large television studios with all technical facilities (approximately 40 television broadcasts and 134 radio programmes per week in 1973). Its tele-news programmes are distributed largely to the south-eastern area of the country. Covering at the moment half of the population of the state of São Paulo, its network is being extended to reach 75 per cent of the state area and 81 per cent of its population.

It transmits on VHF (black and white and colour); its radio station operates simultaneously on long wave, short wave and FM.

In Recife, TV and Rádio Universitária do Recife (Channel 11) belongs to the Federal University of Pernambuco. It was the pioneer educational television station in the country. It is at present planning to become a centre of programme production for the area.

Other components of this public subsystem are: TV Universitária, in Rio Grande do Norte; [1] Fundação Pandiá Calógeras, in Minas Gerais; Instituto de Radiodifusão Educativa da Bahia (IRDEB); Fundação Maranhense de Televisão Educativa (FMTVE), in Maranhão; Fundação Televisão Educativa do Amazonas; Centro Educacional Rádio e Televisão Educativa, in Pernambuco.

The third subsystem is the private system. This is, at present, composed of one organization, the Fundação Educational Padre Landell de Moura (FEPLAM) which, in the state of Rio Grande do Sul, has broadcast cultural and educational television and radio programmes through existing commercial stations.

---

1. The INPE (National Institute for Spacial Research) has been planning the use of a satellite for education for more than five years. Pilot broadcasts are now being tested in Natal (in the north-east) in co-operation with TV Universitária.

4 Mass media and their policies

4.1 Characterization of mass media in Brazil

Information enterprises in Brazil vary as greatly as the country itself. They range from artisanal efforts related to small groups of people (still existing in many places in the interior of the country) to highly sophisticated commercial corporations in the main cities.

Their field of activities are bound by several factors: commercially, they follow the ever-changing market conditions; regarding labour, they are bound by uniform federal laws, especially the Federal Labour Law and the unions. But their main point of reference is the Brazilian cultural context, which varies according to regional patterns.

This explains, therefore, why we must always look at mass media in Brazil bearing in mind the regional influences and characteristics.

4.1.1 Newspapers

The first newspaper published in Brazil, as seen in Chapter 1, was the *Gazeta do Rio de Janeiro,* published by the Portuguese government in exile, in 1808. By 1831 there were fifty newspapers in the country and at the turn the century they were printed in every state of the union. Being the only information media available before radio, newspapers played a most important role in a country of continental dimensions such as Brazil. By 1971, the country had nearly 1,000 newspapers, 233 of which were morning dailies and 28 evening dailies. According to the Brazilian Institute of Geography and Statistics (IBGE), their combined yearly circulation was nearly 1,000 million, that is 3,013,700 per day.

The tendency, however, is for that number to decline sharply due to higher operational costs, the absorption by the electronic media and national magazines of advertising budgets; and due to the reduction in reading-time habits. Although this tendency is most observable in the smaller cities in the interior, important newspapers have stopped operating in the state capitals in the last two years.

The main sources of income for newspapers are advertising and newsstand sales. To survive, advertising space prices must rise, but the result is generally the departure of advertisers for the more productive electronic media, worsening the situation. In the interior, newspapers are generally small enterprises with an average staff of three to fiften people. Medium-sized papers average forty employees. Larger urban papers in Rio and São Paulo average, however, between 1,000 to 3,000 employees.

Technically speaking, most of the small papers, and many of the medium-sized ones, are using obsolete printing methods. In the interior of São Paulo state, for example, half of the newspapers are hand-composed; 95 per cent do not have stereotype plates; 98 per cent have old printing equipment which is difficult and costly to maintain. Only 2 per cent of these newspapers are printed by offset.

Almost half of the Brazilian urban communities have at least one newspaper. Of these, only 547 are regularly produced (dailies and/or weeklies).

As there is no press enterprise with national characteristics, each state has its own key newspapers which, by their editorial positions, strongly influence public opinion, i.e. *O Estado de São Paulo* and *Folhas* in São Paulo, the *Jornal do Brasil* and *O Globo* in Rio, the *Diãrio de Pernambuco* in Recife, *Correio do Povo* in Pôrto Alegre, *Estado de Minas*, in Belo Horizonte, *A Tarde*, in Salvador

More consideration is being given to national newspapers ('national' meaning newspapers with circulation throughout the main state capitals). Distance has been the greatest hindrance. At present, there is a basis for national circulation for the five main newspapers in the country, which are increasingly read in the largest capitals by businessmen and social and political leaders. These newspapers have a national influence over those capable of exerting opinions and taking decisions.

Therefore it can be said that the tendency is for large Brazilian newspapers to develop into national newspapers as technology evolves in the country. As for medium and small papers, the trend is for their reduction in number, as well as an increase in their quality.

The main newspapers in the capitals are morning ones.

Rio de Janeiro and São Paulo have daily papers with circulations above 100,000. However, circulation very seldom surpasses 200,000, with the exception of *O Dia* in Rio and *O Estado de São Paulo* and the *A Folha de São Paulo,* in São Paulo. In the remaining capitals circulation lies between 30,000 and 50,000 issues.

Whereas newspaper circulation outside São Paulo and Rio are lower, it is there that we find the highest number of readers per issue (more than three).

In the southern region of Brazil 70 per cent of readers are male, in the eastern and northern regions 60 per cent, and in the centre (Brasilia) 55 per cent.

4.1.2   *Book publishing*

During the first quarter of this century the number of books published in Brazil was insignificant. The year 1926 registers in São Paulo the publishing of 26 titles (a total of 172,500 copies). During the thirties, almost 2,500 titles were published averaging 5,922 copies each. [1]

In 1940, editors estimated annual Brazilian production at around 8 million copies.

In 1967, 5,618 titles were published, a total of 68,540,000 copies, printing average of 12,200 copies.[2] According to available data, Brazil now leads the field in Latin America.

However as late as 1967, Brazil imported around 9 million dollars' worth of books (50 per cent from the United States of America) and it exported only 500,000 dollars' worth (70 per cent for Portugal).

Today, publishing houses have grown in number, improved their technology and rationalized costs and print runs. The publishing of translated books is vast. Many Brazilian enterprises feel the need to stimulate new local talents for writing: awards and compensations are offered for the best authors; promotion through mass media has improved the selling of Brazilian authors. But the competition with translated books is very stiff.

'The Brazilian book is the only one in Latin America which receives national coverage', says Escarpit.[3] All the states, except two, produce books.

Eighty per cent of Brazilian books are published in São Paulo and Rio de Janeiro, with a slight specialization of the former in didactic and scholarly subjects and the latter predominantly on general culture and literature.

The National Book Institute, an official organization, promulgates a cultural policy for book promotion and distribution covering all fields of interest. Textbook policy is directed by COLTED (National Commission of the Technical and Didactic Book) which distributes books for the elementary level free or at reduced prices. The publishing initiative has to be taken by the publishing house, asking COLTED's agreement. Distribution of such books to school libraries and teachers helps to keep those concerned up to date.

At the University of São Paulo, the same process is observed for science books.

Distribution is the weaker point for the smaller publishing houses; lack of bookshops in many places is solved by the presence of individual sellers or small shops with no proper stock.

1. A. O. Souza, *O Livro Brasileiro*, Maio-Agosto, 1968, Departamento Nacional de Comèrcio, Rio de Janeiro.
2. Fundacão Getùlio Vargas, *Producão de Livros no Brasil*, 1971. (Research sponsored by MEC/BNDE/FGV.)
3. R. Escarpit, *O Livro no Brasil*, 1969. (Unesco report.)

Modernization of the publishing enterprises is a must. The modernized ones (Abril, in São Paulo, for example) sell millions of books and magazines through 14,000 news-stands spread over the country.

4.1.3 *Magazine publishing*

The first illustrated weekly was the *Semana Illustrada*, issued in Brazil in 1900, proceded by numerous humoristic newspapers, short-lived literary and political critical periodicals, which started being published by 1830. Poor printing, inconsistent editorials and small circulations were responsible for the restricted development of the magazine business in the first half of this century.

The situation has radically improved in the last two decades, due to new and powerful enterprises which introduced modern soft- and hardware techniques: controlled circulation, targeted audiences, regional editions, split-runs; offset printing, roto-printing, highly sophisticated colour and design techniques are part of the improvements introduced in both sectors: graphics and magazine marketing.

According to data collected by IBGE, there are 542 magazines published in Brazil, 51.4 per cent with editorial headquarters in São Paulo. Data, however, differ. *Publicity Vehicles* says that 402 is the correct number of magazines published on a regular basis, i.e. that maintain advertising rate lists and pay regular visits to sell advertising space.[1]

The total number of magazine publishers registered in 1972 was forty, the most important are: Abril, Bloch, Vecchi, Rio Gráfica, Efecê, Dirigente.

The Editora Abril is the largest publishing house in Brazil. Apart from its main magazines (*Claudia, Veja, Realidade, Quatro-Rodas*) it has published records, books and has the most diversified production and market techniques.

One of the impressive characteristics of this new approach to printed communications media is the educational and cultural instalment (fascicle) system. The first experiment with this method was the high school television course (São Paulo), specially made to complement educational television transmission (first issue, 150,000), followed by the elementary school radio course, and similar undertakings. The novelty was in the distribution system: 14,000 news-stands throughout the country distributed the materials weekly at an acceptable price.

The system succeeded. Fascicles or collections on philosophy, classical and popular music, painting, science, universal and national literature, arts and crafts, cooking, and so forth, are sold at many points in the country, at the news-stands. Payment systems were also designed to fit the market's psychological and economic characteristics.

---

1. Distribution of magazines is mostly concentrated in São Paulo (38.64 per cent) and Rio de Janeiro (20.72 per cent).

Conveniently adapted, these publications are being exported to Portugal, Spain and Latin American countries.[1]

The Bloch company publishes, among others, *Encilopédia, Pais e Filhos, Joia, Sètimo Cèu,* and the two most dynamic picture magazines: *Fatos e Fotos* and *Manchete.* It is also a diversified enterprise.

Rio Gráfica publishes twenty-six magazines, mostly for children; Vecchi publishes ten, Dirigentes four, and Efecè three magazines each.

Technical evolution, of course, is not a guarantee of growing markets for printed media. Illiteracy, costs, the boom of new titles are pointed to as causes of the printed media market's fragility. Magazines with circulations of over 200,000 per edition are rare. This does not seem to discourage new publications which aim at new types of readers.

The magazine is one of the most important graphic mass media in the country. Distributed throughout Brazil, some of them reach every village more or less at the same time, and have a great influence in the homogenization of behaviour patterns such as language, style, fashion, customs, and so on. Being more permanent than television with a diversified content and pleasant graphic presentation, magazines constitute the basic reading material for a great part of the population.

The trend towards specialized magazines is growing in different segments of the market: for example, those on the home and garden; on children; for the school-teacher, etc. Research and pilot experiments trying to identify new groups of interests will continue.

4.1.4 *Television*

The first commercial television station in Brazil was inaugurated on 18 September 1950, in São Paulo. In 1972, according to ABERT,[2] sixty-four channels were transmitting programmes. Today, although Brazil has 189 television channels, that does not mean that television is being used at its full potential. The number of available channels is 661, according to the Basic Plan of the Ministry of Communication for channel distribution.[3] Of the existing 189 stations, only 59 are generating stations—99 are retransmitters and 31 repetitors. [4] This is due, mainly, to three networks: Rede Globo (twenty stations), Tupi, of the Diários Associados Group (seventeen

---

1. Exports in 1972 amounted to 26,000,000 fascicles, valued at $4.8 million. The figure for 1973, $6 million.
2. Brazilian Association of Radio and TV Enterprises, incorporating the Brazilian Association of Radio and TV, both now grouped under the name of ABERT.
3. O *Estado de São Paulo,* 8 April 1974.
4. According to DENTEL data, São Paulo is the state which has the greatest number of generating stations with a total of eight, followed by Minas Gerais and Rio Grande do Sul (seven each), Paraná (six), Rio de Janeiro (the city) and Malto Grosso (three each), Santa Catarina, Bahia, Ceará, Pará, Maranhão, Piauí, Paraíba, Sergipe and Goiás (one each).

stations) and the Rede Independente—REI (seven stations), which really divide among themselves most of the Brazilian market. The other twelve independent stations, not linked to any television group, transmit programmes only for the city area in which they are located.

Brazil is already able to view directly international programmes and joint network transmissions, due to retransmission facilities via satellite and microwave systems. All stations use the VHF system, except one in the state of Amazonas, which transmits in UHF.

Brazil entered the era of colour television on 31 March 1972, the first programme was presented by seven stations (all in the southern area of the country). Now, even the states of the central and northern areas are transmitting in colour. The 525-line system is used. The PAL colour system has been adopted. Most of the programmes (from soap operas to films, sports, shows) are produced in colour, as is advertising. But the majority of television sets are black-and-white ones.

The number of television sets in the country at the end of 1974 was estimated at 9 million. Official data supplied by Market Research and Planning (MARPLAN) in 1972 estimated 6,500,000 units.

Television and radio stations, as well as all other mass media in Brazil, are traditionally private enterprises, except for a few owned by the government, universities and foundations, even though by law all television and radio stations are considered a federal service, being exploited privately through government concessions (see the National Code of Telecommunications, Section 3.1.2, above).

Three main groups are to be considered in Brazil: the national networks (Rede Globo, Tupi and REI); the autonomous stations, mostly in São Paulo, which generate their own programmes but reach only small audiences; the official stations, generally dedicated to cultural and/or educational programmes.

The networks are formed by stations belonging to groups that own the generating programme stations (the number of which is limited by law) and by affiliated stations that lease the programmes either exclusively or otherwise.

Analytical tables of programming (1974) show that Rio and São Paulo are the main programme generators: daily serials and shows are leased to the smaller stations filling up from 45 to 70.3 per cent of the total broadcast time in other regions. 'Canned' films, specially produced for television, amount to an average of 26 per cent, and the long-run film, up to 11 per cent. Local production (outside Rio and São Paulo) averages 17 per cent.

All urban regions of Brazil are reached by television.[1] Even though each station is considered an isolated unit, most retransmit the programmes

1. Almost 90 per cent of Brazilian homes are within the range of television transmission. However, the ownership of television sets is not homogeneous. Market studies have demonstrated that in the cities, even the very poor families think that television is a must. The television set comes before the purchase of any other home facilities.

generated by two or three main groups,[1] producing a great uniformity of information and entertainment, building an expanding internal market. This fact has been regarded in its positive and negative perspective. Public opinion, the government, as well as small enterprises, feel that the concentration of information power is undesirable, even though some positive aspects of national integration and better production standards have to be considered.

Of the 3,952 municipalities of the country, 2,469 are covered by television; 75 million out of 105 million inhabitants are within the reach of television. Data show that 69 per cent of family units in the capitals and 29 per cent of family units in the interior own television sets. Data also show that the potential audience is estimated around 3.2 viewers per set, averaging 30 million television spectators in all.

In the northern and north-east regions, the municipalities (capitals included) display television at the town's strategic points, so people can enjoy the programmes. This fact increases the potential audience, by making television available to practically everybody, besides supplying the most interesting phenomena of social interaction which is derived from collective reaction to television exposure.

4.1.4.1 *Production of television programmes*

With the exception of some types of children's and women's programmes broadcast during daytime, local news programmes or special editions of sports events, all television programmes are produced and edited in São Paulo or Rio de Janeiro. The serials (films), the most expensive shows and 'telenovels' (soap operas) have their cost absorbed by the other participant stations. Today many programmes of these networks are broadcast via EMBRATEL, in national coverage.

Isolated stations (out of networks) operate with their own programmes and absorb practically the total cost of their production. There are stations specially devoted to certain types of programmes: films, sports, etc. At the major sport events (soccer championships, for example) these stations integrate themselves to the existent networks.

Besides the production of news, shows, serials, television theatre and other types of programmes, some stations sell time to special producers who take the entire responsibility for the programme's style, content and finances. In some cases these producers re-sell the advertising time, or if they are owners of commercial and industrial organizations, their products and services are advertised and often distributed through the programmes.

1. The main network, Rede Globo (1974), has six initiating stations, eleven affiliated stations and eight new stations currently being set up. It is reported to employ 4,500 professionals.

4.1.4.2 *Television programming*

Television programming in Brazil at the peak hours is divided mostly into daily serials, shows, and films or sports, and roughly distributed as follows: 6 p.m. to 8 p.m., serials; 8 p.m. to 10 p.m., shows (and films); 10 p.m. to 12 p.m.,[1] films and/or sports.

During the afternoons, considered as children's hours, programming includes shows and films, with a predominance of films (cartoons, westerns, etc.).

The 1970 census showed that Brazil had 13 million children between 3 and 6 years of age. By law, commercial stations must dedicate at least one hour daily to educational programmes. Some television networks maintain special news programmes for children. The station that does not produce its own educational programmes may obtain them from the educational television's services.

Serials have always existed as a type of programme, but only from 1964 on have they become television's most successful guarantee of audiences and the main source of the stations' income. The serials, because of their capacity to hold large and regular audiences, contributed in the last eight years to the increase of television-cast salaries and to substantive modifications in the habits of thousands of male and female viewers all over the country.

Television shows—humoristic or musical—have been the second most popular type of programme in television, with casts mainly composed of people originally from radio or vaudeville theatre. Important cultural forms have emerged from musicals which are enthusiastically accepted and have been responsible for the mainstream of popular songs as well as sale of records. Auditorium programmes with various forms of competition are also very popular.

Regarding news programmes, they have been improved in the last four years not only in terms of frequency[2] but in journalistic quality. The news events originate in two television centres (Rio and São Paulo) and are transmitted throughout the network-covered areas; provision is made for adding 'on the spot' information. Some networks maintain a body of reporters to cover events all over the country and at the main international centres. Weekly specials (Saturdays, Sundays or special days) give a deeper treatment to information that usually includes news, politics, science, art and other items. [3]

1. Programmes generally last until 12 p.m. or 1 a.m. On Saturdays some television stations broadcast films all night.
2. In 1973, investment in news reporting, coverage of special events, documentaries and films accounted for 42 per cent of the total production costs of the main network (200 minutes of newcasting per day).
3. Special science or art series and special documents on Brazilian regions guarantee large audiences because of a more sophisticated format, greater originality and higher quality performance.

Films have an important place in Brazilian television programming, constituting the basis of many station broadcasts and covering all the gaps in live programming.

The showing of high-quality films is not the rule. Mostly second- and third-class products are transmitted, since the television-film distributor's policy is 'package' selling, which leads to low programming levels.

This type of broadcast has stimulated many debates about the possible effects of imported violence and other negative patterns of behaviour on the Brazilian audiences. The government, teachers, parents and people concerned with the issue have frequently called the attention of the broadcasting directors to films and other programmes that do no stand for people's values and audience uplift. The government has temporarily suspended some programmes as a punitive sanction for the disregard of public good and interest.

4.1.4.3 *Sports broadcasts*

Live and videotape transmissions are current in television weekly programming and have large audiences. Besides national games (mainly soccer), international competitions are regularly scheduled.

4.1.4.4 *Television commercials*

By law, television commercials cannot occupy more than fifteen minutes per hour of programming. By agreement with sponsors, stations have been striving for the improvement of the impact of commercials by lessening their time and by positioning them more strategically. The tendency of advertisers is to buy space in determined programmes and at proper times, according to the target audiences for their messages. This procedure, made possible by the improvement of audience-research techniques, seems to lead to: (a) programming of television channels towards certain types of audiences' caracteristics and preferences, and (b) the optimization of propaganda investments by spotting target audiences. Exclusivity on sponsorship is becoming rare: the common procedure is to give an advantageous opening and closing position for the main sponsor and 'windows' for other announcers.

As a policy of diversification of products communications industry networks are associated to newspapers or organizations for producing records and magazines; for example, the production of sound-tracks for television serials opened up a new field for Brazilian song-writers, whose works became known and were bought by viewing public in Brazil and abroad.[1]

Press criticisms, public opinion and the government are constantly putting pressure on television. There are visible efforts of striving for excellence in their programmes. In addition to conveying more information and better entertainment and instructional programmes, stations often support

---

1. A record catalogue with only thirty titles managed to find a market for almost 2 million copies, which means 33 per cent of all current sales, according to press commentaries (1973).

public services such as educational campaigns, scholarships, sports championships, art exhibits, civic awards, and the like.

4.1.5. *Radio*

The first regular radio station, Rádio Sociedade do Rio de Janeiro, was inaugurated in Rio in 1923. In 1930 only thirteen stations were operating. Over the last forty years, radio has grown as the most important medium for integrative national communication, through its 944 stations, spread all over the country. There is an average of one station for every five counties.

The percentage of family units who own radio sets is high and uniform in the whole country. According to the Manufacturers' Association of Radio and TV Sets (AFRATE) in the capitals 80 per cent of the families own radios; the proportion in the interior reaches 81 per cent.

The federal government has been using radio on a national network system for its daily official information services ever since the middle thirties, and the Ministry of Education uses it for supplementary courses. Radio is considered an important element of diffusion for cultural patterns and standardization of language.

People are used to react to radio in Brazil. This has encouraged station directors to establish policies based on public-opinion research. At the main markets (São Paulo, Rio, Belo Horizonte, Pôrto Alegre) regular monthly research is conducted to measure audience's tastes and preferences. Audience profiles are available at any moment of broadcast, at least in Rio, São Paulo, and the main state capitals.

Audience research became even more important with the advent of television; since the television-station owners were already largely radio-station owners, artistic casts were transferred to television, so were many advertising accounts (the only source of radio income), causing a decline of radio popularity, particularly in the main cities.

This led the radio managers to develop their broadcasts in the direction of target audiences, spotted through research. Radio is again taking a leading position regarding the transmission of news; by conveniently programming its broadcasts, it maintains very high audience levels.

One of the most successful networks broadcasts through thirteen stations in the main capitals. In Rio alone this network has five stations, being distributed as follows: one directed to the mass, popular broadcast; one for 'sophisticated' youth, universitary audience, etc.; one for adults with medium to high incomes, one (broadcasting in stereo) for an élite audience, or refined taste and higher income; and finally one (also broadcasting in stereo) for young people. The system has succeeded and is being used in other markets.

4.1.5.1 *Radio programming*
Popular radio programming is basically made up of music and news, the kind of music and the amount and quality of news being proportional to the

45

target audience that each station aims to reach. News may take from two minutes per hour to three or four hours daily. There is a positive correlation between news broadcast and audience levels.

Programmes destined for women are very much like the women's supplement of Sunday newspapers. Soap operas, radio-post, special sections to answer listeners' questions about problems of health, emotional conflicts, child care, women's rights, etc., are transmitted daily. Radio theatre is also common.

Potential audience, thus, contrary to the general belief, is increasing, mainly due to the transistorized set which is not only cheaper but portable, allowing for listening at most hours of the day. The car radio is another important factor. Manufacturers' figures for radio sets points up this trend.[1]

4.1.6 *Cinema*

'Film is an art, cinema is an industry.' This conception, valid for most contemporary cinematographic production, stresses the role and limitations of cinema as a specific medium of cultural expression in a socio-economic context.

The cinematographic industry in Brazil is still underdeveloped and depends on government support.

Foreign films are thus preponderant in the country, and there is a shortage of specialized professional people in Brazil and a lack of sufficient sound and developing laboratory facilities.

The shortage of specialized professional personnel is being gradually solved. Since 1967, four regular university courses on cinema graduate an average of fifty to seventy new professionals each year in the field of direction, production, editing, photography, script-writing, effects, and so forth.[2]

Laboratory deficiencies constitute a problem too. The two main film production centres (São Paulo and Rio) depend upon a very few laboratories, mostly ill-equipped. This has consequences for technical quality, which in turn results in an additional disadvantage for national motion pictures in competition with foreign productions.

Brazilian films are not legally protected from foreign competition. No extra taxes are imposed on foreign films that enter the country. Such films usually enter the Brazilian market at an average cost of $15,000; Brazilian films cost on average $100,000 which must be covered exclusively by the internal market, since commercialization in foreign countries is unlikely.

1. According to AFRATE the number of transistor radios produced in the country in 1971 was more than 100 per cent greater than the entire radio production of 1963; the car-radio increase for the same year was of 500 per cent. In 1971, 1,646,000 transistor sets and 592,000 car radios were produced.
2. These courses are composed of regular university courses on communication plus professional specialization in cinema. Postgraduate activities (theoretical and technical) are provided at some universities.

In spite of the situation, many culturally expressive films have been made during the last decade. Production has risen to around 100 films per year. But a great number of them have never been exhibited on regular cinema circuits, due to the Brazilian exhibition system.

Foreign film distributors work under the 'package' system, i.e. for each film of proven box-office success, the exhibitor is obliged to accept for showing a certain number of additional films that composes the 'package'. The revenue obtained from the 'package head' is supposed to compensate the exhibition of the whole lot. ('Packages' may vary from six to thirty films). This system keeps the exhibition schedule of the exhibitors quite full, leaving little place for national films.

Instead of imposing extra taxes on foreign films, the policy adopted by the Brazilian Government is to oblige the regular cinema to exhibit national films during a certain number of days per year. In 1939 the policy started with 7 days per year, increasing in 1946 to 21 days; in 1952 to 42 days; in 1963 to 56 days; and 1970 to 112 days. Observance of this law posed many problems and the number is now (1974) reduced to 84 days per year.

The Brazilian producers would like to reverse the situation, i.e. give priority to national films and assign a certain number of days for the high-quality foreign films.

For the moment, 700 foreign films are imported per year, against the national production figure of 100 films. The imported motion pictures to a certain extent inhibit the development of the Brazilian cinematographic industry.

Cinema advertising began, in Brazil, in 1938, based strictly on still transparencies. Between 1940 and 1950 sound and commercials were introduced. Abusive use of these films caused the public to react. In 1953, a municipal law forbad the use of cinema advertising in São Paulo. In 1962, the same happened in Rio. In 1965, a federal law forbid this medium all over Brazil.

In 1966 a new law was promulgated which allows the use of 'filmlets' under the following conditions: projection is allowed at half-light during intermissions (intermissions to be no longer than three minutes) and no film-let can be projected in the same cinema for longer than one week or more than once every six months.

Besides the one- to three-minute 'filmlets' in the cinemas, it is also common to see advertising disguised as 'documentary' films. These are showing the country's industrial progress, new techniques and so on. At the end, a word of thanks is given to the company advertised for its 'co-operation'.

Used in a road-show system, attached to the main films, the use of films for advertising reaches rural areas. As for 'filmlet' production, the advent of colour television has made it grow, since by being usable both in television and cinema, its cost has dropped heavily.

According to the IBGE there were 3,234[1] cinemas in Brazil in 1967, operating under the most varied conditions and subject to diversified living habits.

With a total of 1,909,194 seats the average national audience is 154 persons per show. In the major cities this average grows to 237. This indicates that cinema-going is not yet a very strong habit in the interior.

The advent of television produced a fall in film audiences and the exhibitors tried to attenuate the consequences by upgrading the cinemas, building them with more luxury and smaller capacity, adopting the policy of exclusive exhibitions in one or two particular cinemas, and featuring the cinema as a youthful media, based on research data about youth preferences on entertainment. Exhibition on television of Brazilian films is limited to documentaries and a few feature films, broadcast once a week. There is no regulation regarding Brazilian film exhibition on television.

The history of films in Brazil produces several examples of films as a powerful communication tool. But such films are costly, few, and their messages not always matched with the large audience's tastes and problems; today, the producers' policy is the searching for themes and narrative styles more compatible with the audience's frames of reference, in order to build, step by step, a Brazilian market for Brazilian films.

4.2 Relationship between the mass media and the public

Mass media research is a growing field. The most important research institute is IBOPE.[2] It is said to be the most influential 'art director' of Brazilian mass media, due to the importance placed by radio and television on its audience figures.

Research figures act as a weekly daily barometer of public acceptance or rejection of every programme and determine which alterations should be introduced in them: serials are lengthened or shortened; characters are stressed, modified, introduced or eliminated; plots are made simpler or more complex, depending on research data. Singers, producers, performers, writers and publicity agents, eagerly follow the daily data publication. Salaries and opportunities are directly affected by this data.

1. The National Institute of Cinema estimated the total in 1969 as close to 4,000.
2. Research on communications media in Brazil began with private organizations: the Brazilian Institute of Public Opinion (IBOPE), the Institute for Opinion and Market Research (IPOM), the Institute for Social and Economic Studies (INESE) and Market Research and Planning (MARPLAN). Research has been undertaken by some universities, such as the University of São Paulo, the Catholic University of Pernambuco, the University of Rio Grande do Sul. Private research firms, because of their goals and operational structure, are more able to offer the media data to support their everyday decisions. Research is done for all marketing (and electoral) purposes, by five or six large firms, but quite a number of subsidiary research groups work in the field. These groups are composed mostly of psychologists, sociologists, economists and data analysts. Interviewers are mostly university students. Refined techniques and methods of data collecting and computerization are used.

The media search for favourable public opinion regarding artistes and programmes.

Advertising is a major factor in the socio-economic life of Brazil, since it determines in large measure what happens in the mass media. As no fees are paid by the public for radio and television most of the electronic mass media budget comes from the advertiser, usually through an advertising agency.[1]

There is, of course, a great danger here. Public reaction to programmes leads to the use of cheap and popular foreign 'canned' materials. This is a dangerous way of 'decision-making' about content and format of programmes. It risks retarding the correct use of broadcasting for the cultural development of the people, and the real development of Brazilian mass media.

Thus, mass media are oriented by the audience's behaviour tendencies determined through feedback studies, carried out by audience-research organizations. There is nothing like a Consumers's Protection Institute in Brazil and the limits set for advertising are, in a certain sense, consensual. Government recommendations appear when excesses are considered abusive.

Another important aspect of media-public relationships is the sponsorship of festivals, art exhibits, awards, scholarships, educational compaigns, and the like. In addition newspapers maintain archives and files open to public consultation and students and researchers of all levels can use them.

Recognized professionals from newspapers, radio, television and advertising enterprises are frequently invited as lecturers by the university communication courses. They participate in congresses and other meetings, thus bringing their experience and perspectives into the academic forum. In many communications courses these professionals have become regular teachers.

4.3 Relationship between the media and the sources of information: news agencies

Information sources for media are either their own staff or news agencies.

The most important newspapers and publishing houses maintain their own press agencies. Most of them are holding enterprises which own radio and/or television stations that use the same information.

Among the Brazilian agencies, one belongs to the federal government: the Agencia Nacional (National Agency).

---

1. According to the *Media Yearbook* for 1973, in comparison with 1971, the increase in advertising investments registered in 1972 was 35 per cent. This represents a leap from $430 million to $580 million. In relationship to the GNP, the increase was from 1.15 per cent to 1.19 per cent. The last estimate (for 1973) indicates 1.30 per cent of the GNP was spent on advertising. Of 3,510 milion cruzeiros invested in advertising, about 2,100 milion was channelled through advertising agencies.

Founded in 1946, it is at the moment under the Civil Office of the Presidency of the Republic. It is the central agency of official news and cultural information received through federal, state and local authorities and public and private enterprises. It is based in Brasília, where the information is selected and sent to the newspapers. It has branches in all states and territories.

The National Agency also maintains a television unit in the Federal District, that is able to record, videotape and transmit live directly from a local station, via EMBRATEL, to any television station in the country.

It is in charge of the distribution of government publicity. It runs the *Hour of Brazil*, a daily radio programme broadcast from 7 p.m. to 8 p.m.

The O Estado de São Paulo News agency (São Paulo) is based at the *O Estado de São Paulo* newspaper office. This agency collects news and other materials originating in the country as well as from the foreign correspondents of the *O Estado de São Paulo* and *Jornal da Tarde* newspapers. It distributes news directly to papers in São Paulo, the interior and Brasília. By telex, it distributes news to the main capitals and cities throughout the country. This news is also distributed to the Latin and AFP agencies.

The Folhas agency (São Paulo) services exclusively the Folhas newspaper enterprise but does not sell materials. News gathering is done by around 150 reporters (excluding personnel at the branch offices) who are at the same time the editorial team. The Folhas agency receives material from AP, AFP and ANSA.

The Jornal do Brasil agency (Rio) was founded in 1966. The head office with a staff of twenty-eight is in Rio. This agency receives the foreign service of the *New York Times*, *Los Angeles Times* and *The Economist* (London); its own services supply twenty-eight newspapers and five news agencies and social magazines, and include 30,000 words a day of national and local news in Portuguese, plus features, photos and occasional radio services. Since the enterprise has a governmental concession to run a television channel, the news agency will also supply this new area.

The *Abril* press agency (São Paulo) buys its material from foreign sources for its use (magazines and other publications, except newspapers). It is based at the Documentation Office (DEDOC) of Abril headquarters. It does not maintain a special group for news-gathering, which is done by the Abril editorial team. It has branch offices in all capitals of Brazil and maintains correspondents in Paris, London, Washington, Bonn and Jerusalem; in New York it has a central telex office. It works in connexion with AP and Reuters, on a basis of single material selling.

Other agencies are Transpress (founded in 1958), Meridional (1931), Argus Press (1937) and Asapress (1942).

The main foreign agencies represented in Brazil are AP, UPI (United States), Reuters (United Kingdom), AFP (France), ANSA (Italy), Latin (Latin America) and Tass (U.S.S.R.). DPA, Kyodo and Novosti are also represented.

4.4 Media relationships

Mass media in Brazil are normally owned by large, multi-media enterprises. Their growth in size and complexity was followed by modernization of hardware and techniques (including administration and planning).

Diversification of mass-media enterprises is a continuing phenomenon. 'The selling of information, entertainment and education is business, whichever the system of performance.'[1]

Generally, different media offer support for each other. Television, radio and cinema programmes are advertised through newspapers and specialized magazines. Newspapers also have special sections with features, comments and news about those activities. The audio-visual media use materials and buy information from the news agencies that belong to the newspapers and publishing houses.

Radio and newspapers are traditionally associated. Television follows the same line, with emphasis on image-production—photography, illustrated magazines and cinema. The integration among the media fills all the leisure-time opportunities, mainly in the larger cities. This is carefully planned and controlled.

In the field of education the Free University project is being studied by the Fundação Padre Anchieta (Channel 2) in São Paulo, which will enter the field with a multi-media production programme to cover higher education subjects.

4.5 Trends

A new trend for mass-media enterprises is the optimization of investment of capital and work-force, through diversification outside the media.[2] Uneasiness among small enterprises and reactions from critics have been expressed. Many responsible people feel that a national policy of communication should regulate this expansion.

Newspapers are today squeezed between radio and television on one hand, and specialized magazines on the other. Add to this rising costs of paper, staff, etc., and the 'middle' newspapers are being squeezed out, leaving a few 'great' newspapers and a number of cheaply produced tabloids.

The country's main newspapers will probably develop into a national press as technological improvements allow it to. Public acceptance of such newspapers is already a fact.

1. 'Abril, a Hora de Diversificar', *Propaganda,* Vol. 207 (Year XVII), October 1973, p. 32–3.
2. As an example, from a tourism-magazine base, an enterprise for tourism, including a hotel network, petrol stations, convention and entertainment centres, shopping centres, etc., is being developed.

For magazines, the over-all trend is to follow in quality the technical development abroad. Specialized magazines will continue to fill the gaps within the growing public. Reduction of illiteracy and improvement of general education levels is resulting in increasing numbers of readers, new areas of interest and more sophistication in format and content.

Television is expanding as a presence in Brazilian homes. Educational television is growing and expanding its audiences. After some years of difficulty in the beginning, acceptable patterns—in content, language terms and in rhythm of production—seem to have been reached.

Government support and co-ordination of educational television and radio projects are expected to show positive results in the field.

For the commercial television and radio stations, the trend is to maintain the concession system. There are some signs that television will follow radio, regarding programming diversification, in terms of target audiences.

Radio shows signs of change. Investments in equipment and specialized schooling demonstrate the purpose of adjusting the medium to its new position among the media. Radio has always been a tool for development and national integration. The need for a correct evaluation of its potentiality is being discussed.

5 Professional tradition and training

5.1 Introduction

In Brazil communication work was initially amateur and only later become professional. For the journalists of the empire and the first republican periods, newspapers, the sole mass media then available, were not the principal activities. Low payment turned journalism into a kind of side activity for professionals in many other fields, who found the newspaper a good means to express their opinions and thoughts: lawyers, engineers, sportsmen, writers, people from the theatre, musicians, financial and business circles contributed to the first specialized newspaper sections.

Although not professional journalists, many important names were associated with journalistic activity in the country and these people helped form the roots of reputable corporations and prestigious associations (such as ABI—Brazilian Press Association, which today includes the majority of Brazilian press people).

To a certain extent, the same thing happened with radio and television, with one a marked difference. The journalist in Brazil has always had an aura of heroism and bohemianism, but he was a socially respected (and somewhat terrifying) person because of his education and capacity for expressing opinions. Many of the men and women that came to radio and, later, to television, belonged to the artistic clan, people 'of the night' and 'of the theatre'—those who created and changed things against the general direction and prevailing models as accepted by society. The expression 'people from radio' and 'people from television', are still today—although on a much lesser degree—designations with strong social connotations.

Recently the government has developed a policy for the university preparation of all communication professionals, with the basic understanding that a real policy of communication can only succeed through the performance of the men who work with information.

The existence of university courses for journalism in Brazil dates from thirty years ago. Only in the last decade was the teaching of communication sciences and the preparation of specialized people for the many other communication fields started. This has generated a new kind of professional to fill this developing market.

In 1967 the first comprehensive university schools for professionals of communication were started. Acceptance by the media of newcomers from

53

the university has not been immediate. The situation is now slowly being solved.

The professional register in advertising does not necessarily require a university degree in the field; to be a student in it or to work in an advertising company is enough (Law 57.960 of February 1966). The profession of public relations (Law 5,377 of September 1968) is open to people who have a public-relation university degree or who have been qualified through a recognized course, or worked for enterprises in the field of public relations, before the law was passed. Among communications-media specialities, journalism is the one which has the oldest professional legislation.

At present, in order to be registered as a professional journalist, besides a bachelor's degree in journalism, the candidate is obliged to take a twelve-month probation job in press organization, which can be taken at the last year of graduate study.

'Provisionals' may be admitted where there is a lack of properly prepared university personnel, to the extent of one-third of the jobs available at the enterprise. These provisionals are employees admitted by the press enterprise without satisfying the legal specifications mentioned above. A special law to end the admittance of provisionals by the press enterprises is now before the senate.

Journalism being a profession defined by law, there are special requirements for the curriculum to be taught at the schools, as well as the policy to be followed by enterprises, in terms of payment, working time, social security, and the like. The same applies to public-relations professionals. But for many other communication professions this is not true. Such is the case of television, radio and cinema, areas which are still lacking a comprehensive and clearly defined set of professional requirements, even though many partial approaches already exist.[1]

5.2 Professional training

In the last decade there has been a veritable explosion in communication studies in Brazil. The University of São Paulo's School of Communications and Arts was the first experience (1967) of a global approach to the professional preparation of people to work for media. It now encompasses the

1. Broadcast training opportunities, including courses for radio technicians at secondary level, do exist; higher training in radio and television direction and other related matters is offered at the University of São Paulo, where there is also equipment for colour television training; courses are given as necessary, by the educational television services in São Paulo, Recife, São Luís, Pôrto Alegre, Curitiba and Rio de Janeiro in order to prepare technicians for the media. These cities carry on their own television and radio broadcasts for education. In-service training for these stations is an important task, since education stations cannot compete with the commercial ones, as far as salaries are concerned. Special in-service training courses are also maintained by publishing houses. In São Paulo, the main one has regular training courses for newcomers.

courses of journalism and editing, cinema, radio and television, public relations, propaganda and publicity, tourism and library sciences, besides the courses on art: drama, music and plastic arts. There are now approximately fifty communication schools spread over the country; most of the old schools of journalism have become schools of communication.

Today, the Bachelor's Degree in Communication is divided into a basic and a specialized course. At the University of São Paulo, the basic course gives a background on communication sciences and general culture: theory of communication, mathematics, theory of information, linguistics, sociology and applied sociology; anthropology, psychology and philosophy; research methodology; history of culture and of communications and history of arts; Brazilian culture and Brazilian problems; modern languages; ethics and legislation. In the specialized part of the courses, besides the specific matters taught, training jobs are often performed along with the last year of graduate study. Graduate courses take four years, after which post-graduate courses (two to three years) may lead to the Master's Degree in Communication Sciences or in Communication Arts. The first group of communication graduates left the school in 1971, and the first Ph.D. in Communication Sciences was conferred in January 1973.

When the University of São Paulo started studying the problem of preparing people for the communication professions (then journalism, cinema, radio and television, library sciences, public relations and dramatic arts) the basic curriculum philosophy emphasized the need of a kind of 'integral man', 'to perform one of the most important missions in society'.

This man would be formed through a

clear and contemporary history background; a rigorous methodology of applied linguistics to mass communications; aesthetic and philosophical preparation, plus a knowledge of basic scientific research methods and a special preparation on Brazilian History and problems ... to help the nation overcome underdevelopment. Knowledge about sociology, economy, psychology and politics would complete the basis for the new professional.[1]

Emphasis was given thus to language, literature and history. Scientific background was auxiliary. The curricular inadequacies appeared at the end of the school's first year. Students and teachers understood that the 'integral man' was a much more complex one than first imagined. The true struggle for a 'university school of communications' started at this point.

As a result of this experience, the Federal Council of Education approved the basic curriculum for communication professions, to be used in all Brazilian communications schools, and the approved curriculum was quite different from the experimental one.

Basic communication studies were to take 1,100 class hours and have

1. J. G. Morejon, opening address, first Encounter of Communications Schools, Brasília, 1968.

three main axes: (a) the general culture area (history of culture and communication; history of arts; Brazilian problems and Brazilian culture; philosophy, aesthetics, modern languages, literature); (b) the communication sciences area (communication theory, public opinion theory, mathematical theory of communication; psychology of communication, sociology of communication, anthropology of communication and linguistics); (c) the quantification area (research methodology on communication, statistics, public opinion research).

In 1970 the universities started modifying their old structures to adapt to the credit system. Programmes were modified, didactic habits and models reviewed. The incipient global interdisciplinary approach was largely dropped.

Today, in universities such as Brasília, the students in communication may take their majors in the field, but the university is already organized so that enrolment in other courses and departments is possible and expected. The student must take courses in other areas to fulfil credit requirements.

Some other schools are not as flexible in their structures, and many cannot offer proper training to their students, because of the lack of facilities, laboratories and equipment. Agreements are necessary with the existing newspapers, television and radio stations, organizations and departments of public relations, etc.

There is difficulty in finding adequate teachers, who in many cases are professionals who teachs only part-time.

As personnel prepared by the schools of communication fill media posts, performance feedback will enable a review of contents and teaching methods.

5.3 Labour legislation

Labour legislation defines as a journalist the intellectual worker whose functions range from the search for information to the writing of news, features, and the organization, direction and orientation of such work.

The law also sets the number of working hours (regular hours and overtime), the conditions of performance, working conditions, minimum payment, and so forth.

To be registered as a professional journalist the law requires the presentation of a criminal court affidavit that the person is not being prosecuted or has not been condemned for criminal acts against the national security and proof of Brazilian nationality.

For the professionals who edit publications or maintain news in foreign languages, there is special legislation.

Journalists receive all the benefits that apply to workers in commerce and industry: paid vacations, work-accident insurance, professional-diseases protection, and other related items.

Legislation concerning radio professionals covers fifty-six titles of professions grouped under eleven classes of services, among which: directive activities, speaking, writing, radio theatre, discothèque, sound effects, radio operation, maintainance, electricity—defining the specific functions of each of the fifty-six titles.

The same is true of the television professionals, whose activities are divided into eleven classes—directive activities, script-writing for commercial intervals and audio-hearing, technicians, operators, ciné-television, speaking, artists, telejournalism, auxiliary personnel and administrative personnel— in a total of 116 different functions under which television professionals may be registered.

The law states that for the professionals with journalistic functions (speakers included), five hours is the daily normal workload; for each profession, working time is specified and the worker is protected against delays and other variables that may be time-consuming. Reduction of working time cannot be made unless the worker expressly agrees with it; unpaid professional work is forbidden.

The law also covers the hygienic conditions and social welfare insurance for radio and television workers. There are syndicates of radio and television professionals.

5.4 Syndicates and associations

In Brazil, syndicalization is not compulsory and each class can set its syndicate on a territorial basis which may be district, municipal, inter-municipal, state, interstate or national. The normal basis is the municipal one.

The same law regulates syndicate administration, members' rights and responsibilities, finances and penalties. It also establishes the syndical tax (called syndical contribution) which is compulsory.

People from the mass media maintain their syndicates (each class of workers and owners have their own), through which needs and aspirations are channelled either to the government, in the search of improvements of working and payment conditions, or to the enterprises' owners, for internal subjects. Syndicates maintain juridical departments to handle legal aspects as well as other facilities for their members.

Besides the syndicates, mass media people maintain numerous professional associations. By its prestige (internal and external), the main ones are the Brazilian Press Association and the Brazilian Association of Radio and TV Enterprises. These associations have branches in all states.

The idea of a code of ethics for communication professionals in Brazil has existed ever since the 'heroic' period of the press. Probably, the oldest attempt was the *Prospect*, issued in São Paulo in 1923, dealing with journalistic ethics. Nowadays, an interesting example of a professionial ethics code was proposed at the twelfth National Congress of Journalists (1969). It has a normative structure relating to the role of a journalist within the community, with his sources of information and with his fellow workers. The application of the code is to be the responsibility of journalism labour unions in each state, penalties for violation being established according each union's statues.

An example of the Brazilian code of ethics for mass media is the one approved by the Radio and Television Association which has the following provisions:

1. To use appropriate ethical patterns.
2. To serve community needs and public interests.
3. To search for excellence in the planning and execution of programmes.
4. To emphasize positive stimuli for life and happiness.
5. To care about the good formation of children and youngsters.
6. To banish prejudice about class, race, religion or nationality.
7. To handle with discretion matters being judged by courts or public opinion.
8. To present news with propriety and security, avoiding harm to people's reputations.
9. To avoid sensationalism.
10. To respect the law, to use the right of criticism and inquiry for perfecting law.
11. Not to justify—directly or indirectly—immorality, vice, violence and offence to civism and customs.
12. To maintain the information flow with truth, loyalty and security.
13. To avoid subliminal communication, which is contrary to human freedom.
14. To avoid unfair methods of advertising.
15. To avoid disrespect to old age, and physical and mental disabilities.
16. To avoid themes, texts and dialogues which show disrespect to teachers, parents and the institution of the family.

6 Public participation

6.1 Introduction

Public participation includes the legal right of people to defend themselves from information media (right of response), the public policy about media content, and the many unco-ordinated but constant efforts of individuals, groups and organizations to consider and react to the problems presented by the impact of mass media upon society.

6.2 The right of response

The law guarantees (Article 27) to all persons the right of response and rectification to media comments.

6.3 Public policy

Public communication policy-makers have concerned themselves with quite a number of problems involving the mass communication processes: the amount of foreign material being introduced in the media and its consequences in terms of 'decharacterisation of national culture', and exclusion of Brazilian authors, artistes and producers from the market; the problem of excessive violence, eroticism and other negative patterns in the media; the 'industrial' nature of so-called 'popular music' and other products of media; the pre-fabrication of idols, imposed on the public by multi-media organized campaigns; the low aesthetic quality of some programmes and the danger of information monopoly through ownership concentration. These matters have been raised by public representatives, by government sources and by university studies. It is possible for recommendations and guidelines which influence media programming policies to be issued by the public authorities.

There is not in Brazil an institution like a 'national committee' appointed for systematic work with the mass media or communication matters. For problems which lead public opinion to react, special commissions are usually formed by designation by one of the government branches to study the subject. An interministerial study group was proposed in 1974 within the ministries involved with the subject: that is the ministries of communications, education and culture, and justice.

6.4 The media and the specialized publications and services

Newspapers and magazines, as well as books, intensely discuss media problems, and expose controversial items to public opinion. Publications of interviews, features and research reports, bringing together the contributions of university communication professors and of people that work with the media and other specialists are offered to readers.

Educational television and radio foundations maintained by the state governments, receive numerous suggestions from the public. The Foundation Council is composed of representatives of the most important community groups and public services. Through its members, media administration is supervised. Further controlled reception (in radio and television classes) offers a good opportunity to check audience feedback. Freed from the pressure of the audience-rating indicators and advertising interests, programming has better chances for improvement and a greater range of content selection.

Most of the schools of communication and mass media institutions or enterprises maintain publications on communication.

The approach varies according the institution's main field of activity. For example, the *Jornal do Brasil* publishes *Cadernos de Jornalismo e Comunicação* (Journalism and Communication Notebooks); the Globo network, *Aldeia Global* (Global Village); the University of São Paulo School of Communication and Arts, *Comunicações e Artes* and *Comunicação* (Communication and Arts and Communication); the Bloch Editing House, *Comunicação* (Communication), and so forth.

Institutions of applied communication in the field of agriculture, social service, media agencies and national campaigns also publish magazines, leaflets and bulletins on communication, as well as maintaining special communication services for their audiences and communication training for their personnel.

6.5 School activities

Besides the growth in communication university courses, in the high schools and the teacher's training schools (medium level), special emphasis has been placed on communication problems as a subject for research, features and essays. In colleges communication disciplines are being taught at the schools of administration, economy, education, social sciences, philosophy, linguistics, etc. At all colleges that prepare personnel for services (nursery, for example), courses on communication are available. The universities are frequently asked to organize courses, for the general public or for specialized academic areas that want to get systematized information about communication problems and proposals. The same type of courses are frequently prepared for social agencies such as PTA associations and other organizations, for the cultural improvement of their members.

6.6 Research

As noted above, market research procedures are constantly used in order to detect audience characteristics, not only for programming development but for advertising purposes. Media planning and control is done by auditing of newspapers and magazines circulation (IVC). Surveys on radio and television audiences and sampling of newspaper sales at news-stands (IBOPE) are considered one of the most important indicators of audience trends. Average television audience, minute by minute (Tevemetro); audience profile and reading habits (MARPLAN); specialized checking of competitors' activities (SERCIN); monitoring of controlled radio and television programmes (RTV) are also carried out. There are many organizations which develop special research projects on communication processes for marketing purposes.

6.7 Conclusions

People who are engaged in teaching about communication and mass media, or working with them, are very active in the debate of the important issues brought up by the mass communication processes in society. Schools, associations and private societies hold yearly meetings and seminars in which delegates of the government, mass media enterprises, universities and other interested agencies participate.

Conference recommendations act as feedbacks to guide governmental and business decisions and policies. The government (as well as the Legislative and Executive) is traditionally viewed by the people as a mediating power to solve conflicting interests or situations. In order to achieve efficacy, appeals are sent by individuals, groups or institutions directly to the government or their representatives.

As elsewhere, discussions and questions raised always show a fear of a society entirely programmed through research findings and controlled by the interests behind the mass media; and conversely show the optimistic perspective of a pluralist society where the mass media perform as a dynamic source of the creative process through the sharing of intelligent and relevant information and stimulation of public participation.

7 Conclusions and trends

The first law passed in Brazil (1821) was concerned with freedom of thought, and movement and individual rights and guarantees. The freedom of the press, which was the only mass medium at the time of independence, was thus assured at the time of the formation of the Brazilian State. To preserve it has been a constant concern in everyday socio-political life.

Today, circumstances have imposed a balance between freedom of communication and national order and security. Legislation tries to reconcile these exigences.

'One of the characteristics of contemporary development is the expansion of legal norms', says F. Terrou. This fact is observable in different forms in all countries, as an inevitable consequence of social organization and economic development. The progressive complexity of mechanisms originated by this development, and the need of adjusting them through planning methods, require legal regulations.

Many juridical formulas which are valid for a balanced and developed country demonstrate their insufficiency or even worthlessness in the developing ones. The difficulty of matching ideals, interests and proper policies remains considerable.

The right of the individual . . . conflicts since the beginning, not only with the consolidated interests of groups . . . which divide among them the leadership, but, mainly, with the increased responsibilities of the State which, to reach efficiency in its multiple and interdependent activities . . . is bound to enlarge more and more the circle and the rigor of its control.[1]

Information today is a field particularly touched by technological development. This makes more urgent the development of a communication policy in order to prevent problems of misuse, undue ownership concentration and the like.

Social philosophers pose the question whether institutions and legal norms conceived in the eighteenth or nineteenth centuries, with the objective of giving protection to individual rights of expression against the power of the State, are adequate to deal with information in the era of Telstar, laser rays and industrial concentration of mass media.

1. G. Couto e Silva, *Geopolítica do Brasil,* Rio de Janeiro, José Olímpio Ed., 1967.

Conversely, is the total intellectual and material subordination of communication to the State, which may be successful during a short high-speed developmental period, sufficient for the long-run requirement of enlargement of individual initiative?

A country such as Brazil, engaged in economic growth and national consolidation, can benefit from the accumulated experience of the world, choosing institutions and norms adapted to emerging information technology and the country's real social needs, values and characteristics.

In the process of development there are always more problems than possibilities of solution, more competitors for one cruzeiro of investment than possibilities of satisfaction, more needed products than the ones that can be manufactured, greater demand than availability of specialists. Brazilian infrastructure of communication for development will continue its rapid growth. It can not be seen as 'competing' with other development needs such as industrialization, agricultural modernization, education, public health, development of a sense of nationality, participation in public affairs, or any of the great national objectives of development, since it is a servant and an ally of these problems and projects.

Brazilian society varies enormously in all aspects of development: its regions have a different economy, ecology and way of life. Many communities are fully industrialized, large areas still remain with the most traditional systems of agricultural labour; highly sophisticated and intellectual subcultures coexist with traditional and superstitious ones. Mass media policy envisages serving all: to help the raising of the developing areas and groups to a level compatible with the most developed ones. This must be accomplished in a short time, in order to promote the necessary integration which will enable the best performance of the democratic, pluralist society that has, historically, characterized the Brazilian culture.

The amount of investment in communication as well as the information requirements to match the projected curve of social development must be subject to careful planning. This implies that inside the field of communication priorities must be defined; for example, timing strategies, feedback analysis and alternative programmes as basic decision factors to realistic and efficient operation; and that constant analysis and critical revision assure the validity of the decision-making process.

In conclusion, the hardware aspect of national policy for the use of communication technology in Brazil is well developed and structured. The legal and software aspect need careful study, with the following factors in mind:

A nation's development is a function of a whole set of interrelated changes produced in cultural subsystems and not a product of progress in isolated sectors.

Information involves the fundamental rights of the individual to knowledge and to expression of thoughts and opinions. The Brazilian Constitution explicitly recognizes this. Besides being an individual right, information is also a real social power, '. . . this does not imply that it is a power of the State, but a power within the State'.[1] Information contributes to social and economic development, but this is not an end in itself; the real power of information is the protection and the promotion of human values. This should be one of the main functions of communication policy as a part of the Brazilian general policy of development.

The mass media represent an important development agency, since they affect information and behavioural patterns, develop motivation and create expectations, ideals of performance and ways of life. It is the task of the policy-maker to plan and implement a global policy of communication, which is realistic and related to other development policies. This must be done in a way which will provide the necessary conditions to fulfil the country's values, without frustrating expectations. Above all, it must avoid public deception, which would lead to discrediting social promotion programmes and the sources which originated them.

Messages conveyed through the mass media or other types of communication are subject to distortions relating to the cultural frame of reference, which may be different for the group that sends the messages and the group that receives them; to achieve their objectives, the frame of reference of the receiving group must therefore be understood.

The analysis of variables which compose the intricate processes of social betterment must be done by interdisciplinary teams of specialists from the various areas involved in the development plan, including communications experts.

For Brazilian conditions, the use of advanced technologies of communication for development is essential. The magnitude and complexity of human problems place a heavy and continuous burden on the government, the socio-economic system, the behavioural sciences and the technology of communication. The material and social costs and the calculated risks of the deliberate social intervention projects are enormous. It is urgent that all available resources and data be mobilized; and that priorities of interdisciplinary research be established in terms of human goals, which policy, science and technology should serve.

As noted in preceding chapters, government investment in planning and implementation of communication development has been impressive since 1967. The country has had the benefits of this development, enthusiastically reacting to the new possibilities opened by it.

For commercial ownership of mass media, the trend is to maintain the existing system. Even though a revised National Code of Telecommunications is soon to be approved, thus stimulating possible revisions for other media, the basic philosophy seems to remain.

In respect to television content, the trend is to emphasize national production and develop more rigorous criteria in selecting 'canned' materials. Cinema policies follow the same line.

1. F. Terrou and L. Solal, *Le Droit d'Information*, Paris, Unesco, 1951.

The increasing availability of mass media profesionals prepared by the universities may considerably help in the execution of this policy. This also applies to educational projects which involve mass communication media. The many development plans in various sectors require a national mobilization of human and technical resources for integrated social action.

The Law of Information (Law of the Press), the National Code of Telecommunications and the Law of National Security are the main legal parameters by which decisions about mass media operations and the flow of information are taken. Regulations and recommendations are multiple.

The fact is understandable if we consider that the present Brazilian Government is a revolutionary one. Exceptional measures must be short-term ones and must be seen in a revolutionary context. This means that there is a strong and conscious dynamic interaction between the Brazilian mass media, 'intelligentsia' the government and public opinion, towards a communication policy which equates best, in the field of information, individual goals and constitutional rights, the interests and needs of the media, as enterprises, and the highest objectives and interests for the nation's development as defined by the government's plans and programmes.

There are no ready answers for these problems 'The National Communication Policy-makers must struggle with ideological structures, inevitably engaging in delicate, complex and crucial exercise of harmonization and compromise.'[1]

1. L. R. Beltrán, *National Communication Policies in Latin America,* Bogota, 1974. (Unesco/COM. 74 CONF. 617/2.)

Appendixes

Socio-economic and cultural background of Brazil

Section A: *P O P U L A T I O N*   (at 1 September 1970)

		%
Men	46,331,343	49.7
Women	46,807,694	50.3
Total	93,139,037	

Age groups of population, 1970

	%
0–19	53.0
20–49	36.2
50 and over	10.6

Population estimated for 1974: 105,469,000
Effective workers: 33,500,000

Urban/rural population distribution (percentages)

	Urban	Rural
1950	36	64
1960	45	55
1970	55	45
1980 (projection)	65	35

Population in main cities, 1970

São Paulo,	5,978,977	Fortaleza,	872,702
Rio de Janeiro,	4,315,746	Nova Iguaçu,	731,814
Belo Horizonte,	1,255,415	Belém,	642,514
Recife,	1,084,859	Curitiba,	624,362
Salvador,	1,027,142	Brasília,	546,014
Porto Alegre,	903,175		

Mass media in Brazil

Section A: THE PRESS

Number and circulation of newspapers by states

State or state capital	All newspapers		Daily newspapers				Non-daily newspapers[1]							
	No.	Circulation	Morning No.	Morning Circulation	Evening No.	Evening Circulation	A No.	A Circulation	B No.	B Circulation	C No.	C Circulation	D No.	D Circulation
Rondônia	2	502,000	2	502,000	—	—	—	—	—	—	—	—	—	—
Acre	2	300,039	2	300,039	—	—	—	—	—	—	—	—	—	—
Amazonas	4	7,493,051	4	7,493,051	—	—	—	—	—	—	—	—	—	—
Roraima	1	12,000	—	—	—	—	—	—	1	12,000	—	—	—	—
Pará	11	13,473,106	6	11,727,376	—	—	—	—	5	1,745,730	—	—	—	—
Amapá	3	135,933	—	—	—	—	—	—	2	121,533	1	14,400	—	—
Maranhão	7	2,481,474	4	2,363,674	—	—	—	—	3	117,800	—	—	—	—
Piauí	11	2,109,700	5	1,614,600	—	—	4	482,600	1	9,500	—	—	1	3,000
Ceará	14	9,803,440	5	2,591,680	3	6,909,360	—	—	4	276,400	1	12,000	1	14,000
Rio Grande do Norte	5	3,352,691	4	2,913,502	—	—	—	—	1	439,189	—	—	—	—
Paraíba	7	4,099,521	5	4,079,691	—	—	—	—	—	—	1	4,200	1	19,830
Pernambuco	12	22,103,876	4	18,521,369	1	3,391,607	—	—	5	174,700	—	—	2	12,000
Alagoas	7	2,743,294	3	2,334,894	1	334,400	—	—	2	57,200	1	16,800	—	—
Sergipe	11	1,377,474	3	1,141,074	—	—	—	—	6	234,600	1	600	1	1,200
Bahia	39	27,809,537	3	11,247,088	4	15,381,549	—	—	14	979,200	5	70,400	13	131,300
Minas Gerais	163	134,680,530	12	103,040,270	6	14,631,642	10	6,385,600	81	9,291,368	27	943,350	27	388,300
Espírito Santo	23	5,494,309	4	4,025,859	—	—	4	895,700	10	513,400	3	45,600	2	13,750
Rio de Janeiro	97	311,140,414	33	201,564,574	4	90,346,590	2	763,000	39	17,651,050	8	560,000	11	255,000
São Paulo	353	483,530,826	77	383,019,425	4	47,595,011	39	10,167,900	196	40,377,090	21	1,520,200	16	851,200
Paraná	63	46,226,577	17	35,345,372	2	8,373,755	1	180,000	35	2,176,750	6	133,700	2	17,000
Santa Catarina	45	15,198,259	10	13,335,939	—	—	—	—	33	1,829,920	—	—	2	32,400
Rio Grande do Sul	72	90,865,057	15	79,447,113	1	401,500	13	4,695,994	33	6,173,000	5	81,350	5	66,100
Mato Grosso	25	7,087,125	8	4,379,405	2	1,450,000	6	696,520	8	548,600	1	12,600	—	—
Goiás	11	7,882,143	6	6,081,043	—	—	—	—	3	1,657,100	—	—	2	144,000
Federal District	3	6,317,600	1	5,614,600	—	—	—	—	2	703,000	—	—	—	—
TOTAL Brazil	991	1,206,219,976	233	902,683,638	28	188,815,414	79	24,267,314	484	85,089,130	81	3,415,400	86	1,949,080

1. A = published two of three times a week; B = published weekly; C = published fortnightly; D = other periodicity

Section B: *E C O N O M Y*

GNP *average increase, 1970–74*: 41 per cent

Industrial product increase, 1970-74: 46 per cent

Per capita income 1974: $748

Newspapers by languages, 1971

Language	Number	Circulation
Portuguese	978	1,184,313,566
English	1	4,911,310
German	2	4,283,400
Portuguese and Spanish	1	31,200
Portuguese and French	2	141,500
Portuguese and German	3	11,479,600
Portuguese and other	4	1,059,400
TOTAL	991	1,206,219,976

The number of daily newspaper titles has dropped by about thirty over the last ten years with a corresponding drop of 450,000 in overall circulation figures.

Printers

There are 194 printers, the main ones being located in the major cities. From these, a survey of 125 plants reveals the following concerning printing equipment available: rotaries, 25; offset, 38; letterpress, 50; not specified, 12 (Data from *Propaganda Yearbook*, 1973-74).

Printing personnel

The larger newspapers have an average of 558 employees; medium and small papers, 28 people each. The total estimate of people employed in the newspaper trade is 29,000. Papers such as *O Estado de São Paulo* (and there are five or six of this size) have increased their staff from 1,000 to around 3,000 people. Small papers in the rural areas may employ from 3 to 15 people, the medium-sized papers averaging 40 staff-members each (Data from *Propaganda Yearbook*, 1973-74.)

Newsprint consumption, 1971

Total	Per inhabitant
272,600 tonnes	2.9 kilograms

National newsprint consumption exceeds production (124,400 tonnes). Imports are subject to federal government quoto controls. Newsprint is imported from Scandinavia and Canada. (Data from *Statesman's Year Book*, 1973-74.)

Number and circulation of periodicals by states and state capitals, 1971

State or state capital	Number	Circulation
Amazonas	1	4,000
Roraima	1	20,400
Pará	2	91,200
Maranhão	1	3,600
Piauí	3	8,700
Ceará	5	25,020
Rio Grande do Norte	4	57,300
Paraíba	3	50,500
Pernambuco	3	73,800
Alagoas	1	112,840
Sergipe	6	48,250
Bahia	3	55,640
Minas Gerais	54	4,661,713
Espírito Santo	9	287,700
Rio de Janeiro	237	156,175,100
São Paulo	275	193,772,732
Paraná	31	1,553,825
Santa Catarina	13	541,510
Rio Grande do Sul	42	4,513,915
Goiás	6	101,200
TOTAL Brazil	700	362,158,945

Section C: *B O O K S*

Total number of titles published, 1969:   6,392

Total number of copies, 1972:   161,775,000

Number of libraries, 1968:

National	University	School	Special	Public
1	437	3,804	362	1,717

Book-printing paper consumption: 110 tonnes.

Section D: *RADIO*

Radio transmitters		Wavelength		
	Number	Long/medium	Short	VHF/FM
Commercially-owned[1]	940	835	61	44
Government-owned	54	31	18	5
TOTAL	994	866	79	49

1. Owned by 390 organizations.

Number of radio stations per region (Data from *General Media Review*, 1972)

North	24
North-east	111
South-east	234
South	516
Central-western	59
TOTAL	944

Radio-set distribution

		Region	Absolute numbers
Conventional radio-sets	13,133,242	North	483,562
		North-east	2,479,989
		South-east	4,301,209
		South	5,181,602
		Central-western	686,880
Transistor radios	10,486,727		
Car radios	769,679		
TOTAL	24,389,648		

Percentage of population within range

Eighty per cent of family units in the state capitals have receivers; 81 per cent of family units in the interior have receivers.

Radio-programme distribution

Category	Air time per week (hours)	%
Light entertainment	47,867	52.97
Advertising	17,575	19.44
News and information	13,262	14.67
Broadcasts (special audiences)	7,845	8.68
Arts, letters and sciences	3,418	3.78
Broadcasts for ethnic minorities	407	0.46

Government and private networks' total broadcasting time: 90,374 hours per week.

Radio personnel

São Paulo, 13 stations, 1,500 employees; Rio de Janeiro, 10 stations, 759 employees (networks included). On the basis of a random survey (121 stations in state capitals plus the interior of the country, São Paulo and Rio de Janeiro being excluded) there is an average of 28.41 employees per station.

The total personnel would rise to about 29,078 employees if all stations were taken into account. (*Propaganda Yearbook*, 1973-74.)

In 1971, according to the IBGE, people working in radio broadcasting were distributed as follows:

Administrative	3,083	Technicians	
Writing	2,110	Engineers	100
Artists	814	Middle education	778
Speakers	4,028	Not school	1,697
Workers	3,827		

Section E: *TELEVISION*

Owner groups (1970)

	Stations
Associated dailies and broadcast	20
Globo network	9 (1)
Paulo Machado de Carvalho & Sons	3
Vez Elias Zaran	3
Sirotsky Group	3
Individually owned	18
TOTAL	56

Television stations by regions, 1972

North	5
North-east	11
South-east	18
South	13
Central-western	9
TOTAL	56

Television sets by regions, 1972 (percentages)

North	0.7
North-east	11.4
South-east	72.2
South	11.0
Central-western	2.5

Percentage of families owning television sets in the main cities

São Paulo	81
Rio de Janeiro	94
Belo Horizonte	59
Brasília	70
Salvador	58
Pôrto Alegre	65

In 1972, 65,000 colour television sets were produced.

Television-programme origin

Forty-three per cent nationally produced; imports from the United States and France mainly. All of them receive a Portuguese soundtrack.

Television programme content, 1970

Category	Air time (hours per week)
News and information	1,294
Light entertainment	512
Broadcasts for special audiences	491
Advertising	471
Arts, letters and sciences	291
Broadcasts for ethnic minorities	78
TOTAL	3,137

Or, as seen as a percentage of total air time for the principal Brazilian channels:

	Rio	Pôrto Alegre
News	3	2
Education and culture	15	12
Entertainment	82	86

By 1971 the total broadcasting time had increased to 4,000 hours per week.

Television programmes: weekly distribution by type of programme [1]

Programme type	Minutes	%	
Serials	2,250	11.2	
Shows	2,975	14.9	
Varieties	1,625	8.1	Total entertainment:
Films	6,060	30.4	13,975 minutes = 70.1 per cent
Sports	1,065	5.3	
News	1,125	5.6	
Culture	345	1.8	
Educational	930	4.7	Total information:
Religions	55	0.3	2,855 minutes = 14.3 per cent
Feminine	400	2.1	
Children/youth	3,100	15.6	

1. A comparative study among the existent channels show that they have approximately the same programming line (João Rodol fo do Prado, *Quem vê Quem*, p. 65, Rio de Janeiro, Eldorado, 1973).

Shows, serials and films fill, respectively, 25.3, 27.7 and 27.5 per cent of the total time from 6 p.m. to 10 p.m.

Films fill 51.2 per cent, followed by shows, 20.3 per cent. Educational programmes are concentrated before noon, when they exist at the commercial stations, and before the peak hours at the educational ones.

Average of daily transmission: 9 hours 40 minutes.

Television personnel, 1971

Administrative	1,304
Writers	491
Artists	633
Speakers	275
Workers	2,302
Technicians	
University education	40
Middle education	157
Not schooled	467
TOTAL	5,669

Educational television

Brazilian Central Foundation of Educational FCBTVE (founded 1967). Area of influence: Brazil centre for production and distribution of educational radio and television broadcasts. Linked to the Ministry Education.

Padre Anchieta Foundation (São Paulo radio and television centre) (1967). Area of influence: the states of São Paulo and Espírito Santo, the south-east. Broadcasts range from kindergarten to university level, both instructional and cultural purposes.

University Television and Radio of Recife—Channel 11 (1966). Area of influence: north-east. University extension courses and cultural broadcasts.

University Television of RGN—TV-U (1972). Area of influence: the state of Rio Grande do Norte, North-east. Operates the pilot experiment of satellite education (SACI project).

Pandiá Calógeras Foundation (1971). Area of influence: radio and television for the state of Minas Gerais, south-east (in process of implantation.)

Bahia Institute for Educational Radiodifusion—IRDEB. Area of influence: Bahia state. Broadcasts primarily for elementary education

Maranhense Foundation for Educational Television—FMTVE (1969). Area of influence: Maranhão state, Central north. First-grade schooling.

Amazonas Foundation for Educational Television—TVA (1967). Area of influence: Amazonas state. To complement first-grade teaching and cultural broadcasts.

Centre for Educational Radio and Television—SERTE (1967). Area of influence: Pernambuco state, north-east. Supplementary teaching. Controlled reception from Minerva Project (radio) and High School (television) produced in São Paulo (Padre Anchieta Foundation).

Padre Landell de Moura Educational Foundation—FEPLAN (private) (1967). Area of influence: Rio Grande do Sul, south. Radio and television broadcasts for rural development, general culture, social and civic education, professional education.

Section F: *CINEMA*

Cinema production: imports and exports

Brazil produces an average of fifty to sixty films per year plus short educational and documentary films and news-reels, although the

75

number of major releases in 1970 rose to seventy-two. In 1974, production stayed around 100.

Brazil imports about 700 features a year. These, along with Brazilian feature films, are shown in 2,567 35-mm and 627 16-mm permanent cinemas.

Regions	Number of cinemas	Capacity	Audience
North	60	35,169	10,745,754
North-east	413	186,795	37,220,867
South-east	1,143	643,360	110,785,733
South	1,497	981,602	125,412,183
Central-western	121	62,267	11,312,635
TOTAL	3,234	1,909,194	295,477,772
Capitals	684	635,075	150,545,308

Source: Data on mass media, 1972.

Agencies related to cinema

INC (Instituto Nacional de Cinema), established in 1966, with the responsibility for the internal regulation of imports, distribution, exhibition, licensing, film supplies, etc.

EMBRAFILM—A government enterprise (1969) to encourage the production (through loans and grants) and exportation of films.

INCE (Instituto Nacional de Cinema Educativo), established by a law of 1937 to organize and direct the use of films as an auxiliary means of teaching and popular education.

GCSIA (Gabinete de Cinematografia, Serviço de Informação Agrícola), Ministry of Agriculture, Rio. Produces films on agriculture, cattle breeding and related industries.

Agencia Nacional (National Agency, linked to the Presidency of the Republic). It has produced news-reels and documentaries regularly since 1946. It has its own laboratories.

CNG (Conselho Nacional de Geografia—Brazilian Institute of Geography and Statistics). It produces 35-mm sound films to acquaint the public with the country's different geographical areas, as well as with important events concerning the Council.

Museu de Arte de São Paulo. The museum has been engaged since 1950 in the production of films on art.

Museu de Arte Moderna, which is separate from the Museum of Art, has a library of films classics and is a member of the International Federation of Film Archives. Projections and conferences are organized in its projection hall.

Centro de Estudos Cinematográficos de São Paulo. The centre functions as a film society for the study of cinematographic art. In addition to the projection of films, lectures are organized.

Associação Brasileira Cinematográfica, Rio de Janeiro.

GRIFE deals with 8-mm film production, stimulating the production through a yearly competition.

Section G: *ADVERTISING*

Advertising expenditure by media (percentages)

	1970	1971	1972
Television	38.71	37.62	36.18
Magazines	14.68	13.79	14.12
Newspapers	23.46	24.17	25.21
Radio	14.84	15.36	16.08
Cinema	0.70	0.81	0.92
Outdoor	4.12	4.64	4.66
Others	3.52	3.64	2.83

Bibliography

Books and articles

BELTRÁN, L. R. *National communication policies in Latin America*. Bogotá, 1974. (Unesco/Com. 74 Conf. 617/2.)

CAMARGO, N. The search of a philosophy for the teaching of communication. *Revista comunicações e artes*, no. 6, 1971, p. 49–72.

COUTO E SILVA, G. *Geopolitica do Brasil*. Rio de Janeiro, José Olímpio Ed., 1967.

FOSTER, G. M. *Traditional cultures and the impact of technological change*. New York, N.Y., Harper Bros, 1962.

FREITAS NOBRE, A. *Lei da informação*. São Paulo, Edição Saraiva, 1971.

LERNER, D.; SCHRAMM, W. *Communication and change in the developing countries*. Honolulu, East-West Center Press, 1967.

LOPES, Saint-Clair. *Comunicação e radio difusão hoje*. Rio de Janeiro, Ed. Temário, 1972.

MIRANDA, D. A. *Comentários à lei de imprensa*. São Paulo, Ed. Revista dos Tribunais, 1969.

OPLER, M. E. Developmental change and the nature of man. In: Gallaher, Jr (ed.), *Perspectives in developmental change*, p. 17-35. Lexington, Ky, University of Kentucky Press, 1968.

PYE, L. W. *Communication and political development*. Princeton, N.J., Princeton University Press, 1963.

RODRIGUES, E. C. *Problemas do Brasil potência*. São Paulo, Ed. Unidas, 1972.

SANTOS, R. *Vade-mecum da comunicação*. Rio de Janeiro, Edições Trabalhistas, 1972.

SODRÉ, N. W. *A história da imprensa no Brasil*. Rio de Janeiro, Ed. Civilização Brasileira, 1966.

TERROU, F., SOLAL, L. *Le droit d'information*. Paris, Unesco, 1951.

WESTLEY, B. H. Communication and social change. *ABS, American Scientific Scientist*, vol. 14, no 5, May-June 1971, p. 17–35.

Periodicals

Boletim informativo interno. ABRATE, Brasília.
Boletim informativo mensal. ABERT, Rio de Janeiro.
Cadernos de jornalismo. School of Comm. and Arts. University of São Paulo, 1971–72.
Comunicação e artes. ECA/USP, São Paulo, 1970–72.
Comunicação e problemas. ICINFORM, 1969.

Unidade jornalística. Official publication of the Professional Association of Journalists of São Paulo.

Data sources

Anuário estatístico do IBGE. São Paulo, 1971–72.

Anuário brasileiro de propaganda, Publinform Publ. Informativas S.A., São Paulo, 1973–74.

Panorama geral da mídia no Brasil. 1971.

Mass media in Brazil, Standard Propaganda. São Paulo, 1969.

General media review: Brazil, 1972. Alcãntara Machado Publicidade, São Paulo, 1972.

Book production in Brazil. Research report, MEC/BNDE and FGV, 1971.

Globo annual report. 1973.

O Estado de São Paulo archives.

[B.15] COM. 75/XX.6/A

Date Due

FORM 109

ISBN 92-3-101296-

Communication policies
in **Sweden**

by Lars Furhoff, Lennart Jönsson
and Lennart Nilsson

The Unesco Press

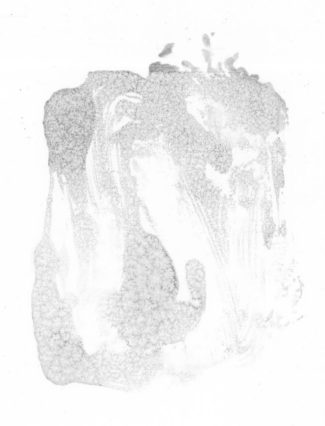